ENTERING THE WAY OF THE BODHISATTVA

T0354248

Entering the Way of the Bodhisattva

*A New Translation
and Contemporary Guide*

Shantideva

TRANSLATED WITH COMMENTARY BY
Khenpo David Karma Choephel

SHAMBHALA

Shambhala Publications, Inc.
4720 Walnut Street
Boulder, Colorado 80301
www.shambhala.com

Cover art: Bodhisattva Avalokiteshvara (after Situ Panchen's [1700–1774]
set of Eight Great Bodhisattvas). Kham Province, Eastern Tibet; 19th
century. Pigments on cloth. Rubin Museum of Art C2008.9 (HAR 65829)
Cover design: Daniel Urban-Brown and Kate Huber-Parker

9 8 7 6 5 4 3 2 1

First Edition
Printed in the United States of America

⊚ This edition is printed on acid-free paper that meets the
American National Standards Institute Z39.48 Standard.
♻ Shambhala Publications makes every effort to print on recycled paper.
For more information please visit www.shambhala.com.
Shambhala Publications is distributed worldwide by
Penguin Random House, Inc., and its subsidiaries.

LIBRARY OF CONGRESS CATALOGING-IN-PUBLICATION DATA
Names: Śāntideva, active 7th century, author. |
Choephel, David Karma, translator.
Title: Entering the way of the bodhisattva: a new translation and
contemporary guide / Shantideva; translated with commentary by
Khenpo David Karma Choephel.
Other titles: Bodhicaryāvatāra. English
Description: First edition. | Boulder, Colorado: Shambhala, 2021. |
Includes bibliographical references and index.
Identifiers: LCCN 2020011932 | ISBN 9781611808629 (trade paperback)
Subjects: LCSH: Mahayana Buddhism—Doctrines.
Classification: LCC BQ3142.E5 C46 2021 | DDC 294.3/85—dc23
LC record available at https://lccn.loc.gov/2020011932

Contents

Translator's Preface

I BEGAN WORKING ON this translation of *Entering the Way of the Bodhisattva* for my own use when teaching from the text or orally interpreting teachings given by my own teacher Khenchen Thrangu Rinpoche. In part, I was curious whether it would be possible to capture in English both the meaning and the musicality of Shantideva's verse. The *Way of the Bodhisattva* has become such a beloved work in India and Tibet not only because it gives such a masterful overview of the path of the bodhisattva. For the most part deceptively simple and direct,[1] Shantideva's language is so evocative and inspiring that the meaning finds its way easily into the heart, not just the intellect. Though I do not have any particular training in verse and can claim to understand Shantideva's work only on a superficial level, the reactions of people I have shown drafts to have encouraged me to think that sharing the results of my experiments more widely might be beneficial.

Yet a translation of Shantideva's text alone would not be so accessible for modern readers, as it is remote in terms of time, culture, and assumptions. Many of Shantideva's ideas may be unfamiliar and contrary to modern thinking, and his allusions and references may make little sense or even be off-putting to contemporary sensibilities without some explanation to contextualize them. Though there are excellent commentaries available in English, it seemed that including a short introduction to the text would be helpful to many readers, both general readers and students of Buddhism. Thus, the book has two parts: the translation of Shantideva's work itself, presented without any embellishment, and an introductory guide intended to give readers a way into the text so that they can begin to appreciate Shantideva's thought.

In preparing the translation, I have followed primarily the canonical Tibetan edition found in the Derge Tengyur. This edition is the basis for a living tradition of explanation and practice that originated with the great scholars of ancient India and came to Tibet with the Indian master Atisha in the eleventh century. It is the version that is most frequently taught and that the greatest number of commentaries use, so it is also the most useful for the greatest number of people. It is also the version that I have been taught on many occasions. However, there is also an extant Sanskrit text, as well as several other Tibetan editions, and I have compared the canonical version against these other versions as I worked. To resolve discrepancies and ambiguities, I usually followed the interpretation in the canonical Tibetan edition, assuming that the Tibetan translators (who always worked in tandem with Indian scholars) are a reliable guide to the meaning. The canonical Tibetan edition appears to have been translated from a different version of the Sanskrit text than the version that has survived, but the two are close enough that lines that are ambiguous in the Tibetan can be clarified by referring to the Sanskrit. I also consulted a variety of Indian and Tibetan commentaries and editions to see which reading is best in terms of the meaning and which seems to come from the most reliable source. I have tried to accommodate the various interpretations found in the commentaries, though that was not always possible. I have also compared my work to several earlier translations of the *Way of the Bodhisattva*.[2] Where I have understood a passage differently, I have checked my own interpretation against the commentaries, never assuming I was right. This translation is built on the foundation of previous translators' efforts, and I am grateful for their work.

Shantideva protests at the beginning of his work that he has no skill in poetry, but his modesty belies his adroitness with verse. Though he largely avoids the florid language and elaborate metaphor commonly found in Sanskrit poetry, he uses rhythm and meter to great effect throughout, mostly writing in light, succinct lines but switching to slightly longer, more measured verse for passages with more gravitas, and in a few spots, to stately long lines laden with imagery. The Tibetan translators followed Shantideva's lead, matching every meter change in Sanskrit with a meter change in Tibetan. They rendered his shorter lines with light, quick, seven-syllable verse and replicated his longer verses with correspondingly longer, more fluid lines.[3] It is clear that the meter—the rhythm—was an important consideration for both Shantideva and the Tibetan translators. Meter is not merely a literary artifice; it also aids in communicating the meaning. Whether expressed in the buoyancy of the Sanskrit[4] or the slight bounce of the Tibetan, Shantideva's lines are crisp, concise, and memorable; they flow easily off the tongue and into memory. They rattle about semiconsciously in the mind and, when a situation arises, pop up as aphorisms reminding us how to think or act. The meter becomes a tool that helps Shantideva's work endure as living words in people's hearts and on their tongues, not merely as dry ink on paper meant primarily for the eyes.

For these reasons, this translation is in unrhymed metered verse, generally matching the line length of the Tibetan and Sanskrit. However, I have allowed more irregularities in the English verse than there are in either the Sanskrit or Tibetan so as to avoid distorting the grammar in ways that might sound affected or old-fashioned to modern ears.[5] There are several instances where (following the example of the Tibetan translators who favored keeping the line length consistent over maintaining the number of lines and who occasionally translated a Sanskrit *shloka* in five lines)[6] four lines of Tibetan are rendered in five or six lines in English, and there is one spot in the eighth chapter where a complete stanza in the Sanskrit and Tibetan would not really stretch to much longer than an English couplet. The hope is that the verse will read naturally but rhythmically, much like the original and the Tibetan translation.

As I worked, I found that, counterintuitively, translating in meter actually helps render the meaning more closely. There is a temptation when translating to add words to clarify meaning, capture nuance, or somehow be more expressive. But sometimes this has the opposite effect and inadvertently clouds the meaning—as the Tibetan proverb says, "The leaves of words obscure the trunk of meaning." Even when it does not, it can encourage readers to engage in inflationary interpretations of the work. Following the stricture of a short, consistent line length forces the translator to consider the author's intent more carefully and convey it economically. The line can then come closer to the original in meaning, pacing, and concision in a way that is more difficult than in prose, where the lack of the external discipline of line length and stress pattern makes it harder to resist when a sentence begs hungrily for more verbiage.

Although, fundamentally, Shantideva sees the equality of all beings, he composed this work in a society with deep biases regarding gender, caste, and so forth. Many of the analogies he uses to illustrate his points reflect ancient Indian culture and, if translated literally, might seem noninclusive or offensive to modern readers, especially with regard to gender. For that reason, when it would have no significant effect on the meaning, I have changed gender-specific language and imagery to be nonspecific. The exceptions include verses where Shantideva refers to customs of his time and changing them would be anachronistic, such as his mention in chapter 8 of women wearing veils, as was the custom in some regions of ancient India. Some terms are left in the masculine, such as the word *king*, as Shantideva and his contemporaries would have expected monarchs to be kings, whether or not historically they actually all were.

The greater difficulty in avoiding gender specificity is the use of third person singular pronouns. Some verses have been recast as plural to avoid the issue, but most often I have used the pronoun *they* as a gender-nonspecific singular pronoun, much as it is used in everyday speech and not infrequently in literary contexts dating back centuries, as any other solution would exclude one gender or another, sound artificial, or be anachronistic. There are a few passages where the pronoun *they* would have been ambiguous; I have used the masculine *he* in those instances, as they mostly refer to despicable people who in Shantideva's time would have been assumed to be male, such as masters who mistreat servants or a king's right-hand man who terrorizes the countryside. My hope is that the ways I have made the translation more gender neutral will be unnoticeable so that readers will not be distracted from Shantideva's main message, which applies to all beings, regardless of the form their bodies take, the proclivities they feel, or the social and cultural situation they are born into.

Though in this preface, I write more about style and form, the substance of Shantideva's thought must be captured if this translation is to serve his purpose in writing this work. Still, if his ideas are to make it past the intellect, the lines that express them must roll and breathe like natural English verse. I cannot judge how successful I have been, but I hope that my efforts make it possible for English speakers to appreciate both the meaning and the feeling of Shantideva's work so that his ideas can enter their hearts.

ACKNOWLEDGMENTS

A book such as this is not the product of a lone individual; it is possible only because of the direct and indirect contributions that many people have made. Foremost are my teachers. Without the teachings and guidance of the Gyalwang Karmapa Ogyen Trinley Dorje, Khenchen Thrangu Rinpoche, and all the other masters who have taught me or given me opportunities to serve, I would have been unable to even begin a translation such as this, and I have tried to incorporate much of what I have learned from them into both the translation and the guide. In particular, Khenchen Thrangu Rinpoche has encouraged me warmly throughout the process and supported me in all ways. My gratitude is likely insufficient to repay the kindness he and my other teachers have shown me. Several people have taken the time to read drafts of both the translation and the guide and to offer many valuable suggestions, foremost among them Josephine Gibson and Lama Zopa Tharchin. I would like to extend my heartfelt thanks to them, as well as to the others who either helped with shorter passages or wish to remain anonymous. Nikko Odiseos of Shambhala Publications has been supportive and helpful through this entire process, and Michael Wakoff has shown both his care for detail and his knowledge of this topic in his attentive editing, giving numerous suggestions that have improved the final product greatly. I am grateful to both of them, as well as to the rest of the staff of Shambhala Publications. Finally, this work would also have been impossible without the generosity of the students and sponsors who support the sangha of Thrangu Monastery, for in supporting the other monks, they have also provided me with food, shelter, and clothing. Despite the help and guidance others have provided, there may still be mistakes and deficiencies, and those are solely my own responsibility. I hope that this book may in some way repay the generosity of all who have had a part in it.

Entering the Way
of the Bodhisattva

Shantideva

In Sanskrit
Bodhisatvacarya avatāra

In Tibetan
Byang chub sems dpa'i spyod pa la 'jug pa

1. Explaining the Benefits of Bodhichitta

I prostrate to all buddhas and bodhisattvas.

1. I prostrate with respect to the sugatas,
Who have the dharmakaya, and their offspring,
And also to all worthy of veneration.
I'll teach in brief, according to the scriptures,
The way to enter the bodhisattva's vows.

2. I won't say anything not said before,
Nor have I any skill in poetry.
Thus I have not intended this for others—
I've written it to cultivate my mind.

3. Meanwhile, this will increase the power of
My faith so that I cultivate the virtues.
If someone else whose fortune equals mine
Should see it, then it may be meaningful.

4. I've gained what is most difficult to get—
The leisures and resources to benefit beings.
If I do not accomplish good while here,
How will I ever come to them again?

5. Just as between the clouds on pitch-black nights,
Lightning reveals the heavens for an instant,
Thoughts of the merits of the world arise
For a rare moment through the buddhas' power.

6. Thus virtues are perpetually weak;
The powers of misdeeds are terribly dreadful.
Besides the wish for perfect enlightenment,
What other virtue triumphs over them?

7. The lords of sages, who have contemplated
For many aeons, see just this will help.
Immeasurable multitudes of beings
Through this will gain the sublime bliss with ease.

8. No one should ever forsake bodhichitta
Who wants to dispel beings' unhappiness,
Vanquish the hundreds of miseries of existence,
And partake in the many hundreds of joys.

9. If they rouse bodhichitta, in an instant
The wretched, fettered in samsara's prison,
Are named the offspring of the sugatas
And revered in the worlds of gods and humans.

10. Just like the greatest kind of alchemy,
It takes this unclean body and transforms it
Into a priceless jewel, a buddha's body,
So firmly grasp ahold of bodhichitta.

11. Examined well by the sole leader of beings
With his immeasurable mind, it has great value.
So you who wish to leave the places of beings,
Firmly grasp hold of precious bodhichitta.

12. All other virtues, like banana trees,
Are spent once they have produced a result.
The tree of bodhichitta constantly
Bears fruit, thus thriving inexhaustibly.

13. Like those who in great danger, rely on heroes,
Why would the careful not rely on that
Which liberates them in a single instant,
Even if they have done horrendous wrongs?

14. Like the inferno at an age's end,
It burns up great misdeeds in a single instant.
The wise protector Maitreya explained
Its countless benefits to Sudhana.

15. To summarize, it's understood
There are two types of bodhichitta:
The mind aspiring for awakening
And engagement in awakening.

16. Just as they know the difference
Between the wish to go and going,
The wise should understand the contrast
Between these two, respectively.

17. Even in samsara, great results
Come from aspiring bodhichitta,
Though unlike engaged bodhichitta,
The merit is not continuous.

18. But from the moment, when for the sake
Of freeing beings in infinite realms,
You truly take up this intent
With irreversible resolve,

19. From that time on, the many powers
Of merit flow forth unremitting
In torrents equal to the sky
Even when you're asleep or careless.

20. The Tathagata himself explained
This and its reasons for the sake
Of beings inclined to the Foundation
In the *Sutra Requested by Subahu.*

21. If someone who benevolently
Intends to merely eliminate
Sharp pains in sentient beings' heads
Possesses immeasurable merit,

22. What need to speak of those who wish
To rid all sentient beings of
Untold distresses and endow
Each one with boundless qualities?

23. Who has such altruism as this?
Does even a father or a mother?
Or do the gods or else the rishis?
Do even Brahmas harbor this?

24. If sentient beings themselves have never
Had such a wish as this before
Even for their own sake in dreams,
How could they have it for another?

25. The wish to benefit beings that others
Have never had for their own sake—
This special jewel of mind—is born,
A wonder without precedent.

26. The cause of every wanderer's joy,
The cure for beings' suffering;
How could one take the measure of
The merit of this precious mind?

27. If merely intending to benefit
Is greater than revering the Buddha,
What need to speak of striving for
The sake of all beings' happiness?

28. They wish to cast off suffering
But rush toward suffering itself.
They wish for happiness, but deluded,
Crush their own pleasure like a foe.

29. For those deprived of happiness
Who suffer many miseries,
This satisfies with every pleasure
And severs every suffering.

30. It also will dispel delusion.
How could there be such good as this?
How could there be a friend like this?
How could there be such merit as this?

31. If to reciprocate a kind deed
Is praiseworthy for a short while,
What need to speak of bodhisattvas
Who do good unsolicited?

32. People extol as doing something good
Those who provide a few with regular meals,
Donating scornfully for a short time
Plain food that satisfies for half a day.

33. What need to speak of those who always give
To beings of untold number for a long time
The sublime happiness of the sugatas,
Fulfilling every one of their desires?

34. Someone who rouses a malicious thought
Toward such a patron, offspring of the victors,
Will dwell in hell as many aeons as
The count of their bad thoughts, the Sage has said.

35. But the results of someone feeling faith
Proliferate in far greater abundance.
With bodhisattvas, even grave events
Don't bring misdeeds; good naturally increases.

36. I prostrate to the bodies of those in whom
This jewel, the sublime attitude, is born.
Even harming them will lead to happiness.
I go for refuge to the wellsprings of joy.

———————

The first chapter, "Explaining the Benefits of Bodhichitta," from
Entering the Way of the Bodhisattva.

2. Confessing Misdeeds

1. In order to grasp that precious attitude,
I make fine offerings to the tathagatas,
To the true dharma, the immaculate jewel,
And to the oceans of qualities, bodhisattvas.

2. As many fruits and flowers as there are,
Whatever kinds of medicine exist,
However many jewels there are in the world,
All clean and pleasant waters there may be,

3. Mountains of jewels and likewise forest groves
In solitary and delightful places,
Bushes adorned with ornamental flowers,
And trees whose branches bow with splendid fruit,

4. Incense and perfumes as from divine worlds
And so forth, wish-fulfilling trees, jewel trees,
And crops that grow without need to be plowed,
All ornaments that are fit to be offered,

5. And lakes and pools bedecked with lotuses,
Where lovely swans have most delightful calls—
Everything that's unowned extending to
The edges of the realms of infinite space—

6. I imagine taking these and offer them well
To the sages, greatest of beings, and their offspring,
Sublime and greatly compassionate recipients.
Think of me lovingly; accept these from me.

7. I am bereft of merit, destitute,
And have no other wealth that I could offer.
May the protectors, who think of others' weal,
Accept these through their power for my sake.

8. Forevermore I offer all my bodies
To the victorious ones and to their offspring.
O sublime beings, accept me entirely,
And I will be your dedicated servant.

9. Because you have accepted me completely,
Not fearing existence, I will benefit beings.
I will transcend my previous misdeeds
And never do another wrong again.

10. Within this sweetly fragrant house for bathing,
Where the bright and lustrous floors are paved with crystal,
Alluring pillars are aglow with jewels,
And glistening pearls are draped in canopies,

11. I bathe the sugatas and bodhisattvas
From precious vases that have been filled full
Of water imbued with many fragrances,
Accompanied by song and harmonies.

12. With cloths that are beyond compare and clean,
Infused with a fine scent, I dry their bodies.
And then I offer them the finest robes,
Well dyed and most delightfully perfumed.

13. I drape Samantabhadra, Lokeshvara,
Manjushri, and the other noble beings
With fabrics that are delicate and soft
And hundreds of the finest ornaments.

14. Like polishing the purest refined gold,
I apply the finest scents, whose fragrances
Waft everywhere throughout the billion worlds,
To the radiant bodies of all sugatas.

15. I offer the great beings I venerate,
The lords of sages, every fragrant flower—
Mandarava, lotus, jasmine, and so forth—
And pleasing garlands strung attractively.

16. I also offer billowing clouds of incense
Filled with the sweetest, most enchanting scents.
And royal feasts I offer them as well,
Replete with an assortment of food and drink.

17. Further, I make an offering of jeweled lamps
Arranged in rows on golden lotuses.
I scatter the petals of attractive flowers
On a paved floor anointed with perfume.

18. I offer those who are compassionate
Numberless palaces adorning the sky,
Beautifully glowing with strings of pearls and jewels
And echoing with melodious songs of praise.

19. I always offer to the lords of sages
Beauteous, jeweled parasols with golden staves,
Fine shaped, upright, and pleasing to the eye,
Their rims festooned with winsome ornaments.

20. And furthermore, may there extend
Clouds of attractive offerings,
With lovely tunes and harmonies,
That soothe all beings' sufferings.

21. May rains of gems and flowers and more
Continuously shower down
On all the jewels of the true dharma
As well as on stupas and likenesses.

22. As Manjughosha and the rest
Make offerings to the victorious ones,
I offer to the tathagatas—
The protectors—and their offspring.

23. I extol the oceans of qualities
With oceans of melodies of praise.
May clouds of hymns in praise of them
Arise just so continuously.

24. I prostrate, bowing as many bodies
As there are atoms in all realms,
To all the buddhas of the three times,
The dharma, and the sublime sangha.

25. I prostrate to the sacred sites
And stupas of the bodhisattva.
I also prostrate to the abbots,
The masters, and the supreme adepts.

26. Until I reach enlightenment's essence,
I go for refuge to the buddhas.
I go for refuge to the dharma
And sangha of bodhisattvas too.

27. To the perfect buddhas and bodhisattvas
Who dwell in every direction—
To those endowed with great compassion—
I join my palms and supplicate:

28. In this and in my other lives
Throughout beginningless samsara,
Deluded, I have done misdeeds.
I've instigated them, and also—

29. Compelled by ignorant confusion—
I have rejoiced in them. I see
They were mistakes, and I confess
To the protectors from my depths.

30. I have, because of the afflictions,
Caused harm with body, speech, and mind
To the three jewels and to my parents
And to the gurus, among others.

31. I, who am wicked and am stained
By numerous failings, have committed
Misdeeds that are most terrible.
Before the guides, I confess them all.

32. I am going to perish quickly,
Before I'm cleansed of my misdeeds.
How can I be rescued from them?
I beg you, please deliver me.

33. The Lord of Death, untrustworthy,
Won't tarry for what's done or undone.
So no one, whether or not they're ill,
Should place their trust in fleeting life.

34. I must leave all behind and go,
But I have not yet recognized that.
For the sake of those I like or dislike,
I have done various misdeeds.

35. Those I don't like will cease to be,
And those I like will cease to be.
I myself will cease to be,
And everyone will cease to be.

36. All of the things that I have used
Will become objects of memory,
As if experienced in a dream.
I'll never see what's past again.

37. Even during this life, many of those
I like and dislike have passed away.
And yet the terrible misdeeds
I've done for their sake remain before me.

38. Because I have not recognized
That I, as well, am ephemeral,
I have committed many wrongs
Out of delusion, greed, and hatred.

39. Not pausing even a day or night,
This life's continuously depleted,
And there is no extending it.
So why would one like me not die?

40. While I am lying in my bed
Surrounded by all my relatives,
I will experience alone
The feeling of my life being cut.

41. When seized by Yama's messengers,
What good are friends? What good are kin?
Merit alone will guard me then,
But I, alas, haven't practiced that.

42. Protectors, I have carelessly
Committed numerous misdeeds
For the sake of this ephemeral life,
Oblivious there is such a danger.

43. If people who are being led
To have their limbs chopped off today
Look different than they did before
With their parched mouths and bloodshot eyes,

44. What need to say how wretched I'll be
When Yama's henchmen have me seized,
Their physiognomies dire and dread,
And I am gripped by terrible pain?

45. "Who will protect me truly from
This horrifying danger," I'll cry,
Eyes bulging with terror, as I search
In the four directions for a refuge.

46. But seeing no protection in
The four directions, I'll then despair.
If there's no refuge in that place,
What will I do at such a time?

47. Thus from today, I'll go for refuge
To the victors, guardians of beings,
Who strive to protect all wanderers,
Those with great power who dispel all fear.

48. Likewise I truly go for refuge
To the dharma they have realized, which
Dispels the terrors of samsara,
And to the sangha of bodhisattvas.

49. Petrified with dread, I give
Myself over to Samantabhadra.
I also make an offering
To Manjughosha of my body.

50. I cry a miserable wail
To guardian Avalokiteshvara,
Whose acts of mercy are unmistaken.
I beg, protect me who have done wrong.

51. To noble Akashagarbha and
To Kshitigarbha, to every one
Of the protectors with great compassion,
I cry from my heart in search of refuge.

52. I go for refuge to Vajrapani,
Upon the sight of whom, from fear,
Malevolent beings like the henchmen
Of Yama flee in the four directions.

53. I have in the past transgressed your word,
But now that I've seen the great peril,
I go to you for refuge and plead:
Swiftly eliminate this fear.

54. If one must do as doctors say
From fear of ordinary illness,
What need to speak of being infected
Continually by the sickness of
The hundred wrongs of lust and such?

55. If even one of these can ruin
All people who live in Jambudvipa
And no other medicine to cure it
Can be obtained in any direction,

56. To think that I might not do as
Directed by the omniscient healer
Who removes every pain would be
Blameworthy and completely deluded.

57. If I must be quite careful of
A minor, ordinary chasm,
What need to mention the abyss
Where I'd fall a thousand leagues for long?

58. It is not right to sit content
And say "I will not die today."
It is inevitable the time
Will come when I will cease to be.

59. Who will grant me freedom from fear?
And how will I escape from this?
I certainly will no longer be.
How can my mind remain at ease?

60. My past experiences are gone,
And what do I have left of them?
But out of my fixation on them,
I've gone against the gurus' words.

61. If I must leave this life behind
Along with family and friends
And go off somewhere else alone,
What good all those I like or dislike?

62. It would be right to only think
In just this way all day and night:
"Nonvirtue leads to suffering.
How can I be freed from it?"

63. Whatever misdeeds I have done
From being ignorant and deluded,
Whether they're naturally unwholesome
Or disobedient misdeeds,

64. Within the presence of the protectors,
From fear of suffering, I join
My palms and prostrate repeatedly,
Confessing every one of them.

65. I supplicate you, guides! Accept
That my misdeeds have been mistaken.
They were not good, and for that reason,
I'll never do such acts again.

———

The second chapter, "Confessing Misdeeds," from *Entering the Way of the Bodhisattva*.

3. Embracing Bodhichitta

1. Delighted, I rejoice in virtue—
Respite from the pains
Of lower realms—and in those who suffer
Dwelling in happiness.

2. I celebrate the virtues gathered
That cause enlightenment.

3. I rejoice in beings' emancipation
From the suffering of samsara,
In the protectors' buddhahood,
And the bodhisattvas' levels.

4. I rejoice gladly in the ocean
Of bodhichitta that brings
All sentient beings to happiness
And gives them benefit.

5. With my palms joined, I implore the buddhas
In all directions: Light
The lamp of dharma in the gloom
Of ignorant beings' woes!

6. Joining my palms, I beseech the victors
Who wish to pass to nirvana,
Don't leave these wanderers in blindness—
Stay for countless aeons!

7. May the virtue I have amassed
By doing all of this
Eliminate all the suffering
Of every sentient being.

8. As long as sentient beings are ill,
Until their ailments are cured,
May I be their medicine, their doctor,
And their nurse as well.

9. May showers of food and drink relieve
The torments of hunger and thirst.
In intermediate aeons of famine,
May I become food and drink.

10. May I be an inexhaustible treasure
For poor and deprived beings
And stay nearby them as the various
Things they need and want.

11. To benefit all sentient beings,
I give without hesitation
My body, my belongings, and
All virtues of the three times.

12. Nirvana's relinquishing everything.
My wish is to gain nirvana.
At some point, all must be relinquished—
It's best to give it to beings.

13. As I have given living beings
This body for their pleasure,
May they always do with it as they like—
Let them kill, revile, or beat it.

14. They may make my body a cause for sport,
Or jest or snickering,
But I have given them my body.
Why bother holding it dear?

15. So let them do whatever acts
Will not bring them any harm.
May thinking of me never be
Meaningless for any.

16. When someone thinks of me and has
A thought of anger or faith,
May that be the cause of what fulfills
Their every benefit.

17. May anyone who slanders me,
Any others who cause harm,
And all who criticize me have
The fortune to awaken.

18. May I be a guardian of the defenseless,
A leader of travelers,
A boat or ship or even a bridge
For those who wish to cross,

19. The land for those who seek the land,
A bed for those without.
For all those beings who want a servant,
May I become their slave.

20. May I be a wish-fulfilling jewel,
Fine vase, accomplished mantra,
Great medicine, a heaven tree,
And bountiful cow for beings.

21. Like earth and the other elements,
Like space, may I always be
The ground, supporting in many ways
The lives of sentient beings.

22. Likewise in all ways for all beings
Out to the edges of space,
May I be, till all pass to nirvana,
What gives them sustenance.

23. Just as the sugatas of the past
Aroused the mind of bodhichitta,
Just as they followed step-by-step
The training of the bodhisattvas,

24. So, too, shall I, to benefit wanderers,
Arouse the mind of bodhichitta.
So, too, shall I follow step-by-step
The bodhisattvas' training.

25. Once the intelligent have thus
Embraced sincerely bodhichitta,
They take delight in their resolve
So that it may continue to grow.

26. My life has become fruitful now.
I've gained this human existence well.
Now I've been born in the buddhas' family
And have become the buddhas' child.

27. From now on I shall always act
In ways that befit my family
So as to bring no blemish on
This stainless, venerable family.

28. Like a blind man who has discovered
A jewel amidst a heap of garbage,
Somehow, by a coincidence,
Bodhichitta has been born in me.

29. This is the great elixir that
Vanquishes the Lord of Death.
It is the inexhaustible treasure
Dispelling the poverty of beings.

30. This is the supreme medicine
That cures the maladies of the world,
A resting tree for beings exhausted
From wandering the paths of existence.

31. This is the universal bridge
That frees all beings from lower realms,
The rising moon of mind that soothes
The torments of sentient beings' afflictions.

32. It's the great sun that brings an end
To the darkness of beings' ignorance.
It is the butter that emerges
From churning the milk of the true dharma.

33. For travelers roaming on the paths of existence,
Desiring to partake of happiness,
This sublime blissfulness is close at hand
To satisfy the supreme guests, sentient beings.

34. Today, in the presence of all the protectors,
I invite all sentient beings as my guests
To buddhahood, and till then happiness.
Gods, demigods, and everyone rejoice!

The third chapter, "Embracing Bodhichitta," from *Entering the Way of the Bodhisattva*.

4. Teachings on Carefulness

1. The victors' offspring who have thus
Grasped bodhichitta steadfastly
Must strive without any lassitude
To never violate the precepts.

2. When something has been started rashly
Or is not properly thought out,
Even if promised, it is best
To examine whether to act or not.

3. But why should I put off that which
The buddhas and their offspring have
Investigated with great prajna
And I myself have also examined?

4. If now that I have made a promise,
I don't fulfill it with my actions,
I will have hoodwinked all those beings,
And what will be my destiny?

5. A person who thinks in their mind
To give some trifling, little thing
But does not give it will become
A hungry ghost, it has been said.

6. Having invited them from my heart
As guests to sublime happiness,
If I deceive all wanderers,
Will I go to the higher realms?

7. People who give up bodhichitta
Still being liberated is
An inconceivable way of karma
That only the omniscient know.

8. This downfall, for a bodhisattva,
Is the most serious of all.
If it occurs, their benefit
To all sentient beings is diminished.

9. Anyone else who thwarts their merit
Even a moment will be born
Endlessly in the lower realms
Since they've decreased all beings' welfare.

10. If one who spoils the happiness
Of even a single being is ruined,
Why mention ruining the well-being
Of infinite beings throughout space?

11. If swinging back and forth between
Strong downfalls and strong bodhichitta,
You mix them in samsaric cycles,
It will take long to reach the levels.

12. Therefore I will, with dedication,
Accomplish what I promised to do.
If from now on, I make no effort,
I'll go from lower to lower realm.

13. Though countless buddhas have appeared
And benefited all sentient beings,
Due to my wrongs, I have not been
A beneficiary of their succor.

14. If I still act in such a way,
Over and over again I will
Experience in the lower realms
Being sick, bound, hacked, and stabbed, and such.

15. It's rare a tathagata appears,
Rare to gain faith, a human body,
And the ability to cultivate virtue.
When will I ever have these again?

16. Although on days such as today,
I may be healthy, fed, and safe,
Life will deceive me in an instant—
This body's a momentary loan.

17. Behaving like this, I will not get
A human body ever again.
If I don't gain a human body,
There's only wrong and never good.

18. If I do not act virtuously
Despite my fortune to do good,
What will I do when stupefied
By the suffering of the lower realms?

19. If I do not perform any virtues
And accumulate misdeeds,
I'll never, for billions of aeons,
Even hear the words "the higher realms."

20. Therefore the Bhagavan taught gaining
A human body is as hard
As for a turtle to stick its neck
Through a yoke tossed on the vast seas.

21. If due to a wrong done in an instant,
One will stay aeons in the Incessant,
What need to say that due to misdeeds
I've done in beginningless samsara,
I will not go to the higher realms?

22. After I have experienced
That much, I won't be freed from there,
For while I am experiencing it,
I will produce still more misdeeds.

23. Now that I've gained such leisure as this,
If I don't cultivate the virtues,
There's no deception other than this,
Nor any greater idiocy.

24. And if, once I have realized this,
I am, deluded, still despondent,
When the time comes for me to die,
I'll feel tremendous grief well up.

25. When the intolerable flames
Of hell have burned my body long,
There is no doubt that blazing fires
Of dreadful rue will wrack my mind.

26. Somehow, by luck, I've gained a place
Of benefit so hard to get.
If I, while I am cognizant,
Am led back to those hells again,

27. It is as if I've been bewitched
By spells and have no will in this.
I don't know what's deluded me—
What do I have inside of me?

28. Aversion, craving, and so forth—
My enemies—have no limbs and such.
They are not brave or wise, and yet
They've somehow made me like a slave.

29. As long as they dwell in my mind,
They'll cause me harm at their own pleasure.
It's wrong to bear that without anger—
Being patient would be blameworthy.

30. If all the gods and demigods
Arose against me as my foes,
They could not take or force me to
The fires of the Incessant Hell.

31. This powerful enemy, afflictions,
Will cast me in an instant there
Where even Mount Meru would be turned
To ash on contact, nothing left.

32. The adversaries, my afflictions,
Last long, without beginning or end.
No other enemy is able
To endure so long a time as them.

33. Everyone, when attended kindly,
Is helpful and will try to please,
But when afflictions are appeased,
They inflict more suffering in return.

34. If thus my long and constant enemies—
The only cause of the proliferation
Of manifold harms—remain within my heart,
Can I be safe and happy in samsara?

35. If the keepers of the prison of samsara,
Such as the murderous butchers in the hells,
Live in the webs of greed within my mind,
How can there be any happiness for me?

36. Therefore, until I see that I have truly slain
This enemy, I will not slacken in my efforts.
Those who are filled with pride, once angered, cannot sleep
Until those who have caused a slight offense are killed.

37. Once the afflicted, who suffer from a mortal nature,
Enter the fray of battle with a strong wish to triumph,
They scorn the pain of being struck by spears and arrows
And won't retreat until they have attained their goal.

38. For me, who strives to vanquish my true, natural foes
That always are the cause of every suffering,
What need is there to say—I won't now be dismayed
Or daunted by the hundred causes of misery.

39. If someone wounded pointlessly by enemies
Will flaunt their scars as decorations on their body,
How then is suffering a cause of injury
For me who truly strives to accomplish a great purpose?

40. If fishermen, outcasts, farmers, and so forth
With only thought of their own livelihood,
Forbear the harms of heat and cold and such,
Why don't I bear with those for beings' weal?

41. When I swore I would free all beings
To the ends of space in all directions
From the afflictions, I myself
Was not yet free of the afflictions.

42. How is it speaking without knowing
My limitations was not insane?
Therefore I'll never be turned back
In subjugating the afflictions.

43. I'll cling to this tenaciously
And enter battle bearing a grudge
Against afflictions other than
The type that conquers the afflictions.

44. It would be better to be slain
By being burnt or decapitated.
In no way shall I ever bow
Before my enemy, the afflictions.

45. Though ordinary enemies, when banished,
Will stay in other lands, which they adopt
To build their power until their return,
The enemy affliction is not so.

46. Wretched afflictions, cast out by the eye of prajna!
When they are driven from my mind, where can they go?
Where can they stay so that they can return to harm me?
It's just that I, weak-minded, have not persevered.

47. Afflictions do not dwell in objects, in the senses, or
    between.
Nor are they somewhere else. Where do they dwell that
    harm all beings?

They're like illusions. Rid your heart of fear, and apply diligence
For the sake of prajna. Why let them torment you pointlessly in
   hell?

48. I've contemplated thus and now will strive
To undertake the precepts as described.
How can a patient who needs medicine
Be cured if they ignore the doctor's advice?

———————

The fourth chapter, "Teachings on Carefulness," from *Entering the Way of the Bodhisattva*.

5. Guarding Awareness

1. All those who wish to keep the precepts
Should concentrate and guard their minds.
If you do not protect your mind,
You won't be able to keep the precepts.

2. An untamed elephant amok
Does not create as much harm here
As letting the elephant of mind
Run loose will cause in the Incessant.

3. The elephant of mind tied tight
With ropes of mindfulness all round,
All dangers will amount to naught;
All virtues will come into your hands.

4. All tigers, lions, elephants,
Bears, snakes, and enemies,
The keepers of the beings in hell,
The dakinis and rakshasas—

5. By binding just this mind alone,
All of these will be bound.
By taming just the mind alone,
All of these will be tamed.

6. For he who spoke the truth has taught
That everything we fear
And sufferings beyond all measure
Originate from mind.

7. Who is it that specifically made
The weapons of the hells?
Who made the ground of burning iron?
Whence come the lovers in hell?

8. The Sage has said that all of these
Arise from wicked thoughts.
Therefore there is in the three worlds
No danger other than mind.

9. If ridding the world of poverty
Made generosity transcendent,
There are still paupers, so how could
The past protectors have transcended?

10. The wish to give all your belongings
And the results to everyone
Is taught to be transcendent giving,
And therefore that is mind itself.

11. And where could fish, et cetera,
Be sent where they would not be killed?
Discipline's taught to be transcendent
From gaining the intent to abstain.

12. How could one kill belligerent beings
Who are as infinite as space?
Vanquishing this one angry mind
Is like defeating all those foes.

13. How could there be sufficient leather
To cover the earth entirely?
With just the leather for my soles,
It is as if the whole earth's covered.

14. Likewise, although I am unable
To keep external things at bay,
I'll keep this mind of mine in check—
What need to ward off anything else?

15. Even with body and speech, results
Of feeble conduct are not like
The fruit of rousing one clear thought—
Rebirth in such as Brahma's Realm.

16. No matter how long they are practiced,
All liturgies and austerities
Are futile, said the knower of suchness,
If something else distracts the mind.

17. Those who don't know this secret of mind—
The sublime, paramount of dharmas—
Want to gain joy and end suffering
But wander to no avail or end.

18. Thus I will grasp and protect well
This mind of mine. This discipline
Of guarding mind aside, why bother
With multifarious disciplines?

19. Like those who in a boisterous crowd
Concentrate and take care of their wounds,
Those in the crowds of evil people
Should always guard the wound of mind.

20. If you are careful of a wound
From fear of its slight, minor pain,
Why not protect the wound of mind
From fear of crushing mountains in hell?

21. Living by conduct such as this,
A steadfast monk who keeps his vows,
Whether in crowds of evil people
Or among women, will not fall.

22. It would be better to lose my things,
Life, limbs, respect, or livelihood;
Better that other virtues lapse
Than ever my intent diminish.

23. I join my palms in prayer and urge
All those who wish to guard their minds:
With all your efforts, please protect
Your mindfulness and your awareness.

24. People who are beset by illness
Have no strength to do anything,
And minds beset by ignorance
Have no strength to do anything.

25. Even if those who lack awareness
Should listen, ponder, or meditate,
It won't stay in their memory,
Like water in a leaky jar.

26. Due to the fault of nonawareness,
Many of those with learning, faith,
And dedicated perseverance
Will be polluted by the downfalls.

27. The robbers that are a lack of awareness,
Following weakened mindfulness,
Will seize the merits you have gathered
While you go to the lower realms.

28. This gang of bandits, the afflictions,
Are seeking opportunities.
Given a chance, they'll plunder virtue
And slaughter life in higher realms.

29. Thus never let your mindfulness
Stray from the gateway to your mind,
And if it goes, recall the pains
Of the lower realms to bring it back.

30. From keeping company with a master,
Instruction from the abbot, and fear,
Those who have fortune and respect
Develop mindfulness easily.

31. "The buddhas and the bodhisattvas
See everywhere without obstruction.
Therefore I always am indeed
Within the presence of them all."

32. Thinking thus conscientiously,
Respectfully, and fearfully,
The recollection of the buddha
Will then arise repeatedly.

33. When mindfulness is stationed there
To guard the gateway to the mind,
Awareness will then also come
And return if it has departed.

34. In every moment, first of all,
I must know if my mind is tainted,
And at that time, I must be able
To hold still like a block of wood.

35. I'll never allow myself to look
Around in purposeless distraction.
With my mind focused, I'll instead
Look always with my gaze cast down.

36. But sometimes I might glance about
To rest my eyes when they're fatigued.
If someone should come into sight,
I'll look at them and say, "Hello!"

37. To know the perils on the road,
I'll look in the four directions often.
Pausing, I first will turn around
Before I look behind myself.

38. Having thus looked ahead and behind,
I'll then proceed or else return.
In every situation, I will
Act knowing the necessity.

39. Beginning endeavors with the thought
"With body, I will stay like this,"
I'll then occasionally examine
"How is my body situated?"

40. With all my efforts, I must check
That the crazed elephant of mind
Has not slipped loose from being tied
To the great post of thoughts of dharma.

41. Exerting myself in samadhi,
I shall examine my own mind
By thinking "What is my mind doing?"
To not lose it for even a moment.

42. If due to danger, feasts, and such,
You cannot, do what's easiest.
It's taught that in a time of giving,
You may ignore some discipline.

43. Once you've considered and begun
A task, don't think of anything else.
Focusing your attention there,
You should accomplish that one first.

44. If you do this, all is done well.
Otherwise neither will get done.
In this way, you will not increase
The near affliction nonawareness.

45. If you engage in idle chat
Or in amazing spectacles
Of various and different kinds,
Give up your eagerness for them.

46. If you should dig the ground, cut plants,
Or draw in dirt without a purpose,
Recall the words of the Sugata
And at that moment, stop from fear.

47. Whenever you have a wish to move
Or else you feel a wish to speak,
Examine your mind first, and then
Be firm in acting properly.

48. At times when my mind feels the lust
Of greed or else the urge of anger,
I must not act and must not speak—
I'll hold still like a block of wood.

49. When I'm excited or else gleeful,
When I feel pride or arrogance,
When I've the thought to dig up faults,
Revive disputes, or be deceitful,

50. At times when I'm intent on boasting
Or being disparaging of others,
When I'm abusive or contentious,
I'll hold still like a block of wood.

51. When I want gains, respect, and fame
Or long for a cortege of servants,
When my mind wants that I be served,
I'll hold still like a block of wood.

52. A wish to give up on others' weal
And seek out my own benefit,
A yen for talk—if these arise,
I'll hold still like a block of wood.

53. And when impatience, laziness,
Fear, impudence, or garrulousness
Or bias toward my own arises,
I will hold still like a block of wood.

54. Thus noticing when their mind becomes
Afflicted or occupied pointlessly,
The heroes use the antidotes
To keep it firmly in control.

55. I will be resolute, full of faith,
Steady, respectful, courteous,
Conscientious, fearful, calm,
And dedicated to pleasing others.

56. I won't despair at the wishes of
The childish who don't get along.
I will be loving, thinking that
Such thoughts are due to the afflictions.

57. Directed by myself and beings
Toward things that are irreproachable,
I'll always keep my mind held fast,
Without a me, like an emanation.

58. Over and over again, I'll think
How after so long I have found
The greatest leisure, and keep my mind
Unshakable as Mount Sumeru.

59. If, mind, you will not be distressed
When vultures lusting for its meat
Together tear the body apart,
Why do you cherish it so now?

60. O mind, why is it that you grasp
This body as yours and guard it so?
If you and it are separate,
Then what good does it do for you?

61. Deluded mind, why don't you cling
To a clean wooden figurine?
How is it sensible to protect
This festering machine of filth?

62. First with your intellect, dissect
And separate the layers of skin.
Dissever with the blade of prajna
The flesh apart from the cage of bones.

63. Then chop apart the bones as well.
Look in as far as to the marrow
And analyze it for yourself.
What essence does it have?

64. If even searching with such effort,
You don't see in it any essence,
Why is it that you still protect
This body in such an attached manner?

65. Its filth is not fit for you to eat,
Nor is its blood fit to drink either.
Its entrails are unfit to suck.
What does the body do for you?

66. Instead, it's logical it be kept
As food for jackals and for vultures.
The bodies of all human beings
Are merely something to be used.

67. Even though you protect it so,
When the merciless Lord of Death
Takes it to give to birds and dogs,
Will there be anything you can do?

68. If you do not give clothes and such
To servants who can't be employed,
Why tire yourself to keep this body
That will, though fed, go somewhere else?

69. Now that you've given it a wage,
Put it to work for your own sake.
Do not give everything to it
If there's not any benefit.

70. Think of this body as a boat,
A mere support for coming and going.
Make it so it fulfills your wish
To benefit all sentient beings.

71. In such a way, be self-controlled,
And always have a smiling face.
Abandon glowering brows and scowls.
Be friendly to beings and straightforward.

72. Do not shove chairs and such about
Impetuously and noisily.
Don't violently open doors.
Always delight in being quiet.

73. Cranes, cats, and burglars move around
In silence, unobtrusively,
To achieve the ends that they desire.
The sages always behave likewise.

74. Ever a student of everyone,
Respectfully accept advice
That's helpful or unsolicited
From those skilled in advising others.

75. To all those who have spoken well,
Say, "You have spoken virtuously."
When you see someone perform merit,
Make them feel glad by praising them.

76. Speak of good qualities discreetly;
Repeat them when they're spoken of.
When someone speaks of your good traits,
Understand they know qualities.

77. All efforts are for happiness's sake,
But even bought with wealth, it's rare.
So I'll enjoy the pleasure of
Delight in the good that others do.

78. For me, there will be no loss here,
And in the next, great happiness.
Wrongdoing brings gloom and suffering,
And in the next, great miseries.

79. When talking, you should speak sincerely,
Coherently, clearly, pleasantly,
Without attachment or aversion,
Gently, and in moderation.

80. When you look at a sentient being,
Think that it's only due to them
That you'll awaken to buddhahood,
And look sincerely, lovingly.

81. Inspired continuously by yearning
Or by the antidotes, great virtues
Are found in the fields of qualities,
Of benefit, and of suffering.

82. Both skillfully and cheerfully,
I'll always do my tasks myself.
I won't, in any of my actions,
Be dependent on anyone.

83. Transcendent giving and so forth
Progress, each greater than the last.
Don't drop the greater for the lesser.
Think mainly of others' benefit.

84. Realizing this, continually
Make efforts for the sake of others.
The merciful, far-seeing one
Allows for them what was forbidden.

85. Sharing with those who've fallen low,
The unprotected, and ascetics,
Eat moderately. Give away
All except the three dharma robes.

86. For minor ends, don't harm this body
That is for practicing true dharma.
By doing so, you'll soon fulfill
The wishes of all sentient beings.

87. Unless your compassionate intent
Is pure, don't sacrifice your body,
But give it as a cause to achieve
Great aims in this and in the next.

88. Dharma should not be taught to those
Who lack respect, who though not sick,
Wear turbans, or hold parasols
Or staves or weapons, or veil their heads.

89. Don't teach the lesser the vast and deep,
Or women unless a man is present.
Approach with equal reverence
Foundational and higher dharmas.

90. Don't introduce a lesser dharma
To those who are vessels for the vast.
Also, do not disregard conduct
Or lead astray with sutras and mantras.

91. Cover it up when you discard
A tooth stick or else when you spit.
It is disgraceful to urinate
And such on usable land and water.

92. When eating, do not cram your food,
Eat noisily, or open mouthed.
Do not sit with your legs stretched out;
Don't rub both arms at the same time.

93. Don't be alone with another's spouse
On rides, beds, seats, or other places.
Observe, inquire, and then give up
All that makes people lose their faith.

94. Don't point at anything with one finger.
Instead, use your entire right hand
To gesture in a respectful way,
Showing the path in such a manner.

95. To give a signal, do not wave
Your entire arm; just move it slightly
And make a noise such as by snapping.
Otherwise it is unrestrained.

96. Like the Protector at nirvana,
Lie down in your preferred direction,
And from the outset, with awareness,
Resolve that you will get up promptly.

97. The bodhisattva's practices
Are taught to be innumerable.
Among them, surely first embrace
The ways of purifying the mind.

98. Three times each day, three times each night,
Recite the *Sutra in Three Sections*.
Because of the buddhas and bodhichitta,
This pacifies remaining downfalls.

99. Whatever you do at any time
Whether for your or others' sakes,
Make efforts to train in the precepts
That have been taught for that situation.

100. There is not anything at all
The victors' offspring should not learn,
And for the wise who live like this,
There's nothing that will not be merit.

101. Do nothing but what benefits
Beings directly or indirectly.
Dedicate solely for beings' sakes
Everything to enlightenment.

102. Even at cost of your own life,
Never forsake the spiritual friend
Who's learned in the Mahayana
And great in the bodhisattva vow.

103. Train in the ways to serve the guru
From the life story of Shri Sambhava.
This and the Buddha's other teachings
Are to be learned by reading sutras.

104. The precepts are described in them,
So therefore you should read the sutras.
As a beginning, you should read
The *Sutra of Akashagarbha*.

105. Because it teaches in detail
What must be practiced constantly,
Over and over again, you should
Read the *Compendium of Trainings*.

106. Or else, for the time being, read
The shorter *Compendium of Sutras*,
And also you should try to study
The two by noble Nagarjuna.

107. What those do not prohibit is
The merit you should act upon.
To guard the minds of worldly people,
Noting the precepts, act correctly.

108. In brief, the characteristic of
Maintaining awareness is just this:
Examine over and over again
The status of your mind and body.

109. With body, I will practice these—
What does just mouthing words achieve?
Does merely reading medical books
Bring benefit to patients?

The fifth chapter, "Guarding Awareness," from *Entering the Way of the Bodhisattva*.

6. Transcendent Patience

———————

1. One moment's anger shatters all
Good acts accumulated
In a thousand aeons, such as giving
Or offering to the buddhas.

2. There is no misdeed like hatred;
No austerity like patience.
So cultivate assiduously
Patience in various ways.

3. When pangs of hatred clutch the mind,
It does not feel any peace.
No joy, no comfort, and no sleep,
No constancy can be had.

4. Even though he has shown them favor
With riches and respect,
Dependents will confront and kill
A master filled with hate.

5. He will distress his friends and kin.
Those gathered with gifts won't serve.
In brief, there is not anything
That makes the angry happy.

6. The enemy anger will create
Sufferings such as these.
Those bent on overcoming anger
Are happy here and elsewhere.

7. When what I do not want is done,
Or my desires are blocked,
Displeasure will then fuel my hatred,
Which will grow to destroy me.

8. Thus I'll destroy the sustenance
Of this, my nemesis.
Other than causing harm to me,
This enemy has no function.

9. Whatever happens, I will not
Upset my cheerfulness.
Displeasure won't fulfill my wishes
But strip away my virtues.

10. If something can be fixed, what need
Is there to be displeased?
If something can't be fixed, what good
Is it to be displeased?

11. We don't want pain, humiliation,
Insults, or disrepute
Either for us or for our friends.
It's the opposite for our foes.

12. The causes of happiness are rare;
The causes of pain are frequent.
Without pain, there's no wish for freedom,
So, mind, you must be steadfast.

13. The Durga cults and Karnatans
Pointlessly bear the sensations
Of burns and wounds, so why am I
A coward for freedom's sake?

14. There's nothing at all that is not easy
If you are used to it.
By getting used to minor pains,
You'll bear great harms as well.

15. Don't I see this with pointless pains
Of serpents and mosquitoes,
Of feelings of hunger, thirst, and such,
And rashes and so forth?

16. Thus I won't be thin-skinned about
Heat, cold, and wind and rain,
Or illness, bondage, beatings, and such—
Being so makes them worse.

17. Some, seeing their own blood, become
Exceptionally courageous,
And some, on seeing another's blood,
Will faint and fall unconscious.

18. This is from steadfastness of mind
Or else from cowardice.
Thus disregard the injuries—
Do not let pains affect you.

19. Though pain occurs, the wise do not
Disturb their joy of mind.
When waging war against afflictions,
Harm's plentiful in battle.

20. Triumphant heroes are they who
Ignore all pain and quash
Hatred and such—the enemy.
Everyone else kills corpses.

21. Plus, suffering has benefits:
Weariness dispels arrogance;
Compassion arises for the samsaric;
Shunning misdeeds, you delight in virtue.

22. We don't get angry at bile and such,
Great sources of suffering,
So why be angry at the sentient?
Conditions provoke them too.

23. Just as such illnesses occur
Involuntarily,
Afflictions are compelled to arise
Involuntarily.

24. Though people don't think, "I'll get angry,"
The commonplace angers them.
Though they don't think, "I shall arouse it,"
Their fury still arises.

25. All the offenses that there are,
All manifold misdeeds,
Occur because of their conditions—
They have no self-control.

26. And the assembly of conditions
Has no thought "I'll produce,"
Nor does what it produces have
The thought "I'll be produced."

27. The primal substance that they claim
And self that they imagine
Do not think, "I will come to be,"
And arise intentionally.

28. Without arising, they don't exist—
What then would want to arise?
Always distracted by an object,
It also would never cease.

29. If permanent, the self, like space,
Would clearly have no action.
When it encounters other conditions,
What acts on the unchanging?

30. If during the action, it's like before,
What does the action do to it?
If you say, "This is what acts on it,"
What is it that's related?

31. In this way, everything's dependent
And thus has no control.
When you know that, you won't get angry
At any illusory thing.

32. "Who averts what? Even averting
Would be illogical."
It's logical to say suffering
Will cease, dependent on that.

33. Thus when you see a friend or foe
Acting improperly,
Think happily that this occurred
Because of such conditions.

34. If things were accomplished by free will,
No living being at all
Would ever have any suffering,
For no one wants to suffer.

35. They injure themselves by being careless
Of thorns, et cetera.
From lust, they starve themselves and such
For sake of sex and the like.

36. Some hang themselves or jump from cliffs,
Take poison or eat poorly,
Or behave unmeritoriously,
Causing themselves harm.

37. When overcome by the afflictions,
They'll kill their own dear selves.
At such a time, how would they not
Cause harm to others' bodies?

38. Though rarely do we feel compassion
For those who kill themselves
And so forth when afflictions arise,
What good is getting angry?

39. If causing harm to others is
The nature of the childish,
Anger at them is as senseless as
Resenting fire for heat.

40. But if the fault is adventitious
And beings' natures are gentle,
Anger at them would not be right,
Like begrudging the sky for wafting smoke.

41. If I, ignoring the main thing—
The stick—get angry at its wielder,
Who is impelled by ire, it's right
To get incensed at hatred.

42. I, in the past, have caused such harms
To other sentient beings,
So it is right these ills occur
To me who have hurt beings.

43. Their weapons and my body both
Are causes of suffering.
They wield the weapons, I the body.
With whom should I get angry?

44. Blinded by craving, I have grasped
This human body-like blister
That, prone to pain, can't bear being touched.
Whom to get mad at when it's hurt?

45. The childish don't want suffering,
But thirst for suffering's causes.
Can I resent another being
When harmed by my own wrongs?

46. If like the guardians of hell
And like the sword-leaf forests,
This is produced by my own actions,
At whom should I get angry?

47. If those who, goaded by my karma,
Appear and do me harm
Should go to hell because of that,
Have I not brought them ruin?

48. Because of them, I'll purify
My many misdeeds through patience.
Because of me, they'll go to hell's
Long-lasting agonies.

49. If I am causing harm to them
While they are helping me,
Why, O cruel mind, do you get angry
Mistakenly at them?

50. If I've the quality of intention,
I will not go to hell,
And what can happen to them now
If I protect myself?

51. But if I harm them in return,
They will not be protected
While my own conduct is debased;
Austerity destroyed.

52. Because the mind's not physical,
No one can wound it at all.
Because of fixation on the body,
The body is harmed by pain.

53. Contemptuousness, abusive speech,
And words that are unpleasant
Inflict no harm upon the body.
Mind, why do they incense you?

54. Displeasure others show for me
Will not devour me
In this or in another life.
So why do I dislike it?

55. Though I do not want that because
It blocks material gain,
I'll leave my things behind me here,
While wrongs will long remain.

56. It's better I die now than live
Long with wrong livelihood.
Even were I to live for long,
The pain of death's the same.

57. Someone feels bliss a hundred years
In a dream and then wakes up.
Another experiences bliss
A moment and then wakes.

58. For either of the two who wake,
That bliss will never return.
A long life and a short life both
Are finished when we die.

59. Though we acquire many things
And enjoy them a long time,
We will go as if robbed by bandits—
Naked and empty-handed.

60. If I live off my gains to abate
My wrongs and practice virtue,
Won't anger for the sake of goods
Waste virtue and be a wrong?

61. And if the purpose of my living
Itself should be debased,
What good's this life when all I do
Is to commit misdeeds?

62. Those who disparage you harm beings
So you get angry, you say.
Why don't you also get upset
When others are disparaged?

63. If losing faith depends on others
So you forgive the faithless,
Afflictions depend on conditions,
So why not forgive your critics?

64. It's not right to get angry at those
Who insult or destroy
Statues, stupas, and the true dharma—
The buddhas and such aren't harmed.

65. As taught above, see those who harm
Your master, kin, and friends
As doing so from circumstances
And thus stave off your anger.

66. If both the sentient and nonsentient
Cause harm to living beings,
Why single out and resent the sentient?
Forbear their harms instead.

67. Some, being ignorant, do wrong.
Some, being ignorant, get angry.
What would make either innocent?
Which of the two is guilty?

68. Why in the past did they do acts
That would make others harm them?
Since everything depends on karma,
Why hold a grudge for the other?

69. Realizing this, no matter what,
I will endeavor at merits
So everyone will come to have
Mutually loving thoughts.

70. When fire that has burned one house
Spreads to another home,
You gather up and throw away
The straw and such that fuel it.

71. Likewise throw away instantly
Whatever you're attached to
That fuels the fires of hatred, fearing
It will consume your merit.

72. What's wrong if someone condemned to death,
Their hand cut off, is freed?
What's wrong with human suffering
Removing you from the hells?

73. If I cannot bear this amount
Of suffering in the present,
Why then do I not stop my anger,
Cause of hell's agonies?

74. For sake of desire, a thousand times
I have experienced
Being burned and such in hell but done
No good for myself or others.

75. But this is not that great a harm,
And a great aim will be accomplished.
It's right to only be delighted
At pains that dispel harm to beings.

76. If others are pleased when they praise someone
As having qualities,
Why then, O mind, do you not as well
Praise them and take delight?

77. Your pleasure from rejoicing is
A blameless source of delight
Allowed by those with qualities—
The best way to gather others.

78. "But others will be happy too."
If you don't want this joy,
You've stopped paying wages and will thus
Destroy the seen and unseen.

79. When yours are the qualities described,
You want that others be pleased.
When others' qualities are described,
You don't want to be pleased yourself.

80. If you roused bodhichitta because
You want all beings to be happy,
When beings find themselves happiness,
Why does that make you angry?

81. If you want for beings the buddhahood
Adored in the three worlds,
Why does it gall you so to see
Them have some paltry honor?

82. If a relative whom you support—
Someone to whom you give—
Should gain a livelihood, would you
Be angry instead of pleased?

83. If you don't want even that for beings,
How can you wish them enlightenment?
If you are irked by others' wealth,
How can you have bodhichitta?

84. If they get something or it remains
Inside the patron's house,
In either case, it is not yours.
Given or not, why care?

85. Why do you throw away your merits,
Your faith, and qualities?
Tell why you're not angry at the one
Who doesn't hold on to their gains.

86. Do you not only feel no sorrow
For the wrongs you've done yourself
But also want to vie against
Those who have performed merit?

87. Even when enemies are displeased,
What's there for you to enjoy?
The wishes in your mind alone
Won't cause them any harm.

88. How would it please you to accomplish
The pain you wish for them?
You say you would be satisfied—
What greater ruin than that?

89. Unbearably sharp, the hook cast by
The fishermen, afflictions.
Caught on it, surely I'll be cooked
In cauldrons by hell's keepers.

90. Praise, fame, and honor will not beget
Merit or a long life.
They will not bring me strength, good health,
Or physical well-being.

91. If I know what is good for me,
What's good for me in those?
If all you want is mental pleasure,
Use drink and dice and such.

92. For sake of fame, some squander wealth
Or even get themselves killed.
What use are words? When you are dead,
Who will they make happy?

93. When their sand castles are destroyed,
Children wail in distress.
Likewise when I lose praise and fame,
My mind is like a child's.

94. Words have no mind; for them to wish
To praise me is impossible.
Though hearing that another likes me
May be a cause of pleasure,

95. What good does someone else's fondness
For me or another do me?
That like and pleasure is their own;
I won't get even a bit.

96. If their being happy makes me pleased,
I should be so for all.
Why aren't I pleased when they're made happy
By their love for another?

97. Therefore my pleasure that arises
When I am being praised
Is irrational and nothing more
Than just a child's behavior.

98. Praise and so forth bring distraction,
Destroy world weariness,
Cause envy of those with qualities,
And ruin prosperity.

99. So haven't those who lurk nearby
To wreck my acclaim and such
Come to protect me against falling
Into the lower realms?

100. What need have I, who seek liberation,
Of the fetters, gain and respect?
And why should I get angry at those
Who release me when I'm bound?

101. When I want to rush into suffering,
How is it I get angry
At those who, as if blessed by the Buddha,
Don't let me, blocking the way?

102. It makes no sense to get angry at those
Who I think thwart my merit.
If there's no austerity like patience,
Should I not dwell in that?

103. If I cannot be patient with them
Because of my own faults,
Then all I've done is block the cause
Of merit that was at hand.

104. If the cause of something is that which
If absent, it won't be,
And with which, it will come to be,
How is that called an obstruction?

105. A beggar appearing at the right time
Does not prevent your giving.
It is not right to say your abbot
Stopped you from going forth.

106. Though there are beggars in this world,
Those who cause harm are rare,
For if you do no harm to others,
No one will harm you back.

107. Therefore just like a trove appearing
Painlessly in a home,
I will delight in enemies,
My friends in enlightened conduct.

108. Since they and I created it,
It's right to give the fruits
Of patience to my enemies first,
For they're the cause of patience.

109. If enemies deserve no honor
Since they've no thought to make you patient,
Why would you honor the true dharma,
The cause of accomplishment?

110. Though you won't honor your enemies
Because they want to harm you,
If they, like doctors, wished to help,
How could they make you patient?

111. Thus since malevolent intent
Is what produces patience,
Just they are the cause of patience and worthy
Of veneration, like true dharma.

112. These are the fields of sentient beings
And victors, said the Sage.
Many who have respected them
Have gone beyond to perfection.

113. A buddha's qualities are gained
From beings and buddhas alike.
How is it right to have respect
For victors but not beings?

114. It's not from qualities of intention
But due to the results
That beings have qualities like theirs
And therefore are their equals.

115. Offering to those with loving-kindness
Is sentient beings' greatness.
The merit of having faith in the buddhas
Is the buddhas' greatness.

116. For gaining a buddha's traits, they have
A part and are thus equal.
Infinite oceans of qualities,
The buddhas are equaled by none.

117. Offering even the three realms
To those who appear to have
A tiny share of the qualities
Of those who are the unique
Collection of sublime qualities
Would be inadequate.

118. Since beings have a part in the birth
Of a buddha's supreme traits,
They're similar to that extent
And thus deserve veneration.

119. Other than pleasing sentient beings,
What way is there to repay
Those stalwart friends who act to bring
Immeasurable benefit?

120. Since helping them repays those who forsake
Their bodies and go to the Incessant Hell,
Even when they inflict on you great harm,
Make all your actions solely excellent.

121. Meanwhile, how is it I—an ignoramus—
Am prideful and don't act like a true servant
To those for whose sake they who are my lords
Have disregarded even their own bodies?

122. Making them happy, whose happiness delights
And injuries distress the lords of sages,
Brings all the lords of sages gratification,
While harming them brings injury to the sages.

123. Just as no object of desire will bring
Happiness when your body is on fire,
If you harm sentient beings, there is no way
That those with great compassion could be pleased.

124. Therefore I now confess all my misdeeds,
Which, as they have caused harm to sentient beings,
Distress all those endowed with great compassion.
May all those whom I have displeased forgive me.

125. To please the tathagatas, from today onward
I shall be the world's slave. I won't strike back,
No matter how many people stomp my crown
Or kill me. Guardians of the world, be happy!

126. There's no doubt they whose nature is compassion
Regard all of these beings as themselves.
Those who are seen as sentient beings in nature
Are guardians in essence—why disrespect them?

127. Just this is what will please the tathagatas.
Just this is what fulfills my very own aims.
Just this dispels the sufferings of the world,
And therefore I will always do just this.

128. Just as, when one of the king's men
Wreaks havoc on many people,
Even if able, the farsighted
Do not retaliate

129. For he is not alone—his forces
Are the forces of the king—
Likewise do not look down upon
Weak people who cause harm,

130. For theirs are the forces of hell's keepers
And of the compassionate.
Just as his subjects propitiate
A tyrant, respect beings.

131. Even if angered, could a king
Inflict what is experienced
Because of making beings despair—
The agonies of hell?

132. Even if pleased, a king could not
Provide what is achieved
By making sentient beings happy—
Buddhahood itself.

133. Leave future buddhahood aside,
Do you not see in this life
That pleasing sentient beings brings
Much glory, fame, and joy?

134. While in samsara, patience brings
Beauty and so forth,
Good health, prestige, a very long life,
And a chakravarti's pleasures.

———

The sixth chapter, "Transcendent Patience," from *Entering the Way of the Bodhisattva.*

7. TEACHINGS ON DILIGENCE

1. Thus with patience, be diligent.
Enlightenment dwells in striving so.
There is no motion without wind;
No merit without diligence.

2. Diligence is a zest for virtue.
What's contrary to that? To explain,
It's laziness—clinging to the bad
And sloth and self-disparagement.

3. Laziness arises from
Not wearying of samsaric pain,
From craving sleep and savoring
The pleasures of being indolent.

4. Stalked by the hunters, the afflictions,
You've walked into the trap of birth.
Yet do you still not understand
You've entered the maw of the Lord of Death?

5. Have you not seen that your compeers
Are being killed, one after another?
Still, even so you fall asleep,
Just like a buffalo with a butcher.

6. When all around the ways are blocked
And the Lord of Death is watching you,
How is it you enjoy your food?
How can you like so much to sleep?

7. You will die soon, so until then
Gather the accumulations.
For then, when there is no more time
To give up sloth, what will you do?

8. This is undone, this just begun,
And this remains but halfway done.
The Lord of Death will suddenly come,
And you will think, "Alas, I'm finished!"

9. You'll watch your relatives lose all hope
As tears from shock of grief roll down
Their faces, their eyes red and swollen.
You'll see the faces of Yama's henchmen.

10. Recalling your misdeeds with anguish
And hearing the din of hell, the dread
Will make you foul yourself with filth.
You'll be in torment—what will you do?

11. If like a living, writhing fish,
You have such terror in this life,
What of the intense suffering
Of hell from the misdeeds you've done?

12. Your flesh is tender when it's touched
By scalding water, yet you have done
The karma of the hottest hells.
Why do you stay so comfortably?

13. You want results without any effort—
Such pain for one so delicate!
When grasped by death, you're like a god.
Alas! Suffering will destroy you!

14. Free yourself with the human boat
From the great river of suffering.
Such a boat is hard to get again.
Now is no time for sleep, you fool.

15. Forsaking the sublime joy of dharma,
The cause of infinite delight,
Why do you relish such distractions
And games that will cause suffering?

16. Don't be discouraged; practice with
The forces, purpose, and self-control:
The equality of self and others
And exchanging yourself for others.

17. Don't get demoralized and think,
"How is it I could be awakened?"
For the Tathagata who speaks
The truth has spoken truly thus:

18. If they should rouse the strength of effort,
Even gnats, mosquitoes, bees, and worms
Will gain what is so hard to achieve—
Unexcelled enlightenment.

19. If I, born in the human race,
Can recognize what helps and harms
And don't give up enlightened conduct,
Why wouldn't I reach enlightenment?

20. "But I'm afraid of sacrificing
My limbs and such," I say, not thinking
What is severe and what is light—
Delusion has left me in fear.

21. For countless millions of aeons,
I will be hacked and stabbed and burnt
And rent asunder many times,
But not achieve enlightenment.

22. The suffering for me to achieve
Enlightenment, though, has a limit,
Like pain from an incision made
To excise a painful foreign object.

23. All physicians cure disease
Through the discomfort of a treatment.
Therefore put up with small distress
To overcome myriad sufferings.

24. The Supreme Physician does not use
Commonplace treatments such as those.
He cures unfathomably great diseases
With the most gentle of remedies.

25. Initially, the Guide prescribes
Giving away vegetables and the like.
Eventually, when used to that,
You will be able to give your flesh.

26. For once you understand your body
To be like vegetables and such,
What difficulty would there be
In relinquishing your flesh and such?

27. There is no pain from giving up wrong,
No melancholy from being wise,
For harm to the body is from misdeeds
And harm to the mind from misconceptions.

28. If physical pleasure is from merit
And mental pleasure from being wise,
Would the compassionate despair
To stay in samsara for others' sake?

29. Because the power of bodhichitta
Exhausts one's misdeeds from the past
And gathers oceans of merit, it's taught
That they surpass the shravakas.

30. So ride the horse of bodhichitta
That banishes all weariness.
Who in their senses would be lazy
To go from one joy to the next?

31. To benefit beings, the forces are
Longing, steadfastness, joy, and deferring.
Longing is born of fearing suffering
And contemplating its benefits.

32. Thus give up what is contrary.
By force of effort and mastery
Of longing, pride, joy, putting aside,
Strive to increase your diligence.

33. My own and others' infinite wrongs
Are mine indeed to eliminate,
But every single fault will take
An ocean of aeons to extinguish,

34. And I don't see that I've begun
To exhaust them even the slightest bit.
Infinite suffering is my lot;
Why does my heart not burst apart?

35. My own and others' numerous
Qualities are for me to accomplish,
And though each quality will take
An ocean of aeons to cultivate,

36. I've never cultivated even
A fraction of a quality.
It is astounding how I've squandered
This birth that somehow I've achieved.

37. I haven't worshipped the Bhagavan
Or given the pleasures of great feasts.
I have not acted for the teachings,
Fulfilled the wishes of the poor,

38. Provided safety to those in fear,
Or given comfort to the wretched.
All I've created is suffering
And pain inside my mother's womb.

39. Because I have not longed for dharma,
Such tribulations have occurred
To me before and even now.
Who would forsake the wish for dharma?

40. The Sage has said the basis of
Everything virtuous is longing.
The root of that is meditating
On the full ripening of results.

41. Sufferings, unhappiness,
Dangers of assorted types,
And deprivation of desires
Occur because of committing misdeeds.

42. Wherever they go, those who perform
The virtue that their heart desires
Will be welcomed with offerings
Resulting from their acts of merit.

43. Wherever they go, those who commit
Misdeeds, though they want happiness,
Will be destroyed because of their wrongs
By the weapons of suffering.

44. From virtues, you will dwell within the heart
    Of a vast, cool, and fragrant lotus flower,
Where nourished by the pleasing voices of
    The victors, you will grow in majesty.
And when, because of light rays from the sages,
    The lotus blossoms, you will then emerge
Before the victors with a supreme body—
    You will become a child of the sugatas.

45. But from your many nonvirtues, the henchmen
    Of Yama will entirely flay your skin,
And you will be most miserable and wretched.
    Then molten copper melted over the most
Intense of fires will pour all over your body,
    And blows rained down by blazing swords and spears
Will hack your flesh into a hundred pieces,
    And you will fall onto the burning iron ground.

46. Therefore you should long for virtue
And cultivate it with dedication.
Once started, meditate on pride
With the methods from the *Vajradhvaja.*

47. Examine first your resources
And then begin or don't begin.
Not starting may well be the best;
Do not turn back once you've begun.

48. For with that habit, in other lives
Misdeeds and suffering will increase,
Or else the time of the result
Will be diminished, unaccomplished.

49. Be prideful of these three: your acts,
Afflictions, and ability.
To say, "I shall do this alone,"
Is in itself the pride of action.

50. The worldly, overcome by afflictions,
Cannot accomplish their own good.
Beings are not as able as I,
And therefore I'll do this myself.

51. How can I just sit there when
Another does the menial work?
If out of pride, I won't do that,
It's best for me to have no pride.

52. When it encounters a dead snake,
Even a crow acts like a garuda.
When I myself am weak, a downfall—
Even if small—will cause me harm.

53. Can there be freedom from privation
For the disheartened who have stopped trying?
It's hard for even the great to best
Those who have roused their pride and effort.

54. Therefore with a steadfast mind,
I'll vanquish downfalls. If instead
They conquer me, my wish to triumph
Over the three realms is laughable.

55. I'll be victorious over all.
I will let nothing vanquish me.
A child of the lion, the Victor,
I shall abide within such pride.

56. Those beings whom pride has subjugated
Do not have pride; they are afflicted.
They have succumbed to the foe pride—
The proud are not controlled by foes.

57. Inflated by afflicted pride,
That pride will lead you to lower realms,
Destroying the feast of being human.
A slave who feeds on others' scraps,
You will be stupid, ugly, and weak.

58. You'll be reviled everywhere.
If wretched folk inflated with pride
Are also counted among the proud,
Do say, then, what the lowly are like.

59. Those who grasp pride in order to defeat the enemy pride,
They are the proud, the victorious who are themselves the heroes.
The ones who thus destroy the growing enemy of pride
Will perfect the result of victory that beings desire.

60. Amidst the crowd of the afflictions,
Persevere in a thousand ways.
Like lions with jackals, do not let
The hosts of the afflictions strike.

61. No matter how great the danger is,
People always guard their eyes.
Likewise when you are in grave peril,
Do not fall under afflictions' control.

62. It's better to be burnt to death
Or have my head decapitated—
Never in any way shall I
Bow to the enemy, affliction.

63. Likewise in every situation,
I'll never act any way but right.

64. Like wanting the pleasure that results
From play, they are enchanted with
The acts that are for them to do—
Delighted, never satisfied.

65. We act for sake of happiness,
Not knowing whether pleasure will come.
How can all those whose deeds are pleasure
Be happy if they do not act?

66. If you aren't sated by desires,
Which are like honey on a razor,
How can you then be sated by merit,
Whose ripening is peace and pleasure?

67. So therefore to complete your task,
Immerse yourself in action, like
An elephant scorched in midday sun
Who sees a lake and plunges in.

68. But when your strength diminishes,
Put work aside to act again later.
Once it's well done, leave it behind—
Look forward to the next and later.

69. Like parrying the enemy's blade
When you are in the thick of battle,
Evade the weapons of afflictions,
And strike the foe afflictions hard.

70. If you should drop your sword in battle,
You'd swiftly pick it up from fear.
If you lose mindfulness—your weapon—
Take it up quickly, fearing hell.

71. Just as a poison spreads throughout
The body through the flow of blood,
Likewise if they can get a chance,
Your wrongs will spread throughout your mind.

72. Practitioners should concentrate,
As fearful as someone holding a bowl
That brims with oil before a swordsman
Who threatens death if any spills.

73. So just as you would spring up quick
If a snake should get into your lap,
If sleep and slothfulness should come,
Then counteract them with great haste.

74. For every single wrong that occurs,
Chastise yourself and ponder long,
"However I can, I'll make it so
This never happens to me again."

75. "In circumstances such as this,
How shall I practice mindfulness?"
With that as cause, you should seek out
A meeting and appropriate action.

76. Before you act, no matter what,
To have the strength for everything,
Recall the words on carefulness
So that you will be light and nimble.

77. As tufts of cotton are directed
By wind as it moves to and fro,
So, too, is all accomplished under
Direction of enthusiasm.

———————

The seventh chapter, "Teachings on Diligence," from *Entering the Way of the Bodhisattva*.

8. Teachings on Meditation

1. After thus rousing diligence,
Settle your mind into samadhi.
A person whose mind wanders perches
Between the fangs of the afflictions.

2. With solitude of body and mind,
Distraction won't occur.
So you should thus forsake the world
And also give up discursive thoughts.

3. You won't renounce the world if attached
Or else if you crave goods and such.
In order to abandon those,
The wise should contemplate like this:

4. Realizing that afflictions are destroyed
By shamatha and insight in conjunction,
First seek out shamatha, which comes from joy
For having no attachment to the world.

5. Who is someone ephemeral
To cling to the impermanent?
In a thousand lives, you'll never see
The ones who were so dear to you.

6. Not seeing them, you'll feel no joy.
Your mind won't rest in equipoise.
Even seeing them won't be enough—
Craving will plague you as before.

7. Being attached to sentient beings
Obscures completely the true nature
And wrecks world weariness as well.
Grief will torment you in the end.

8. Because you only think of them,
Your life will pass by pointlessly.
Inconstant friends and relatives
Will ruin even constant dharma.

9. Acting the same as childish folk,
You'll surely go to the lower realms.
They lead you to unsuitable states—
What good's the company of fools?

10. One moment, friends, but in the next
They're enemies. They are incensed
By what should please them. It is hard
To gratify ordinary beings.

11. Angered by talk of what is helpful,
They turn me away from my own welfare.
If I don't listen to their words,
They'll go to lower realms, enraged.

12. They're jealous of superiors;
Competitive with their own equals.
They're proud toward their inferiors
And arrogant when they are praised.
When you reproach them, they get angry.
When is there benefit from the childish?

13. When you keep company with the childish,
You praise yourself, belittle others,
Talk of samsara and such with them—
Nonvirtue inevitably occurs.

14. In this way, my associating
With them will only bring me ruin.
They will not bring me benefit,
And I won't benefit them either.

15. Flee far away from childish folk.
Be friendly when you do meet them,
And without getting too familiar,
Dispassionately behave well.

16. Just like a bee with flower nectar,
I'll only take for dharma's sake
And live unacquainted with anyone,
As though I'd never seen them before.

17. "I get a lot and am respected;
Many people are fond of me."
If you cling to conceits like these,
You will face terrors after death.

18. The passions of a deluded mind,
Whatever it may be they are for,
Are multiplied a thousand times
To then rise up as suffering.

19. Therefore the wise do not desire.
It's from desires that fear arises.
They'll be discarded naturally,
So understand this and be steadfast.

20. Even if you gain many things
And become popular and renowned,
It is uncertain where you'll go
Along with all those goods and fame.

21. When someone else disparages me,
What joy is there for me in praise?
When someone else is lauding me,
Why be displeased when I am slandered?

22. If even buddhas cannot please
Beings with various inclinations,
What need to speak of a wretch like me?
Thus I will give up worldly thoughts.

23. They revile people who get nothing
And speak ill of those who get much.
What pleasure comes from those whose nature
Is to be hard to get along with?

24. As the tathagatas have said,
No childish being is a friend
Because unless it suits their purpose,
The childish are not gratified.

25. In forests, animals and birds
And trees don't speak disparagingly.
When is it I will live together
With them, whose company is pleasant?

26. When will it be that I can stay
In caves or in abandoned temples
Or under trees, not looking back,
And not attached to anything?

27. When will it be that I can dwell
In places naturally vast
That no one owns where I can act
In freedom and without attachment?

28. When will I keep a plain alms bowl
And such, and clothes that no one wants?
When will I live free from all fear
Even if I don't protect this body?

29. When will I go to charnel grounds
To see that other people's bones
And my own body are the same
In being perishable things?

30. This body of my very own
Will also become just like those
Whose stench is such that even jackals
Will not come anywhere close to them.

31. This body is born all alone,
And if the flesh and bones born with it
Will fall apart, be strewn about,
What need to speak of other friends?

32. At birth, it's born alone; at death,
It dies alone. If no one else
Can take a share of the pain, what good
Are loved ones who make hindrances?

33. In the same way as travelers
Take lodging when they're on the road,
Those on the pathways of existence
Take lodging in a place of birth.

34. Up to the time when four pallbearers
Would carry it away from there
While people mournfully lament,
Till then I shall go to the forest.

35. With no friends and no grudges either,
This body'll stay in solitude.
Considered as if dead already,
There'll be no mourners when it dies.

36. With no one seated at my side
To cause disturbances and grief,
There's no one to distract me from
Recalling the buddha and so forth.

37. Thus I'll remain in solitude,
In the delightful atmosphere
Of joyful forests with few hardships,
Where all distractions are quieted.

38. Relinquishing all other thoughts
And with one-pointed mental focus,
I'll strive to settle my mind down
In equipoise and to subdue it.

39. In this world and the next one too,
Desires will lead you to your ruin.
Here they bring killing, bonds, and wounds,
And in the next, the hells and such.

40. The one for whom you earlier
Made many requests through go-betweens,
For whose sake you did not refrain
From misdeeds or even from disgrace,

41. For whom you put yourself in peril
And also used up all your wealth,
The one whose tight embrace would bring
The highest pleasure is nothing but

42. A skeleton—not anything else.
What you have lusted for and clung to
Has no control, is not a self.
Why don't you go to nirvana instead?

43. You first took pains to lift her face,
But she then bashfully looked down.
Whether you'd seen it before or not,
It had been shrouded by a veil.

44. The thought of it afflicted you,
But now her face is visible—
You see what vultures have revealed,
And why does it now make you flee?

45. You guarded it so closely from
The glance of anyone else's eyes.
Why don't you, who are so possessive,
Protect it when it's being eaten?

46. You see the pile of flesh that vultures
And other animals devour.
Would you give someone else's food
Garlands, perfumes, and jewelry?

47. Seeing it as a skeleton,
You're frightened, though it does not move.
Why aren't you scared when, like a zombie,
It's animated by something else?

48. You lusted for it when it was covered,
So why not when it is uncovered?
If it will serve no purpose, why
Would you embrace it when it's covered?

49. Since both saliva and excrement
Are made out of the very same food,
Why of the two do you dislike
Excrement and yet like saliva?

50. Not even taking pleasure in
A cotton pillow soft to the touch,
The lustful say it exudes no stench.
They are deluded about filth.

51. Though cotton may be soft to touch,
Deluded, lowly, lustful people
Get angry over it and say
That it's unable to make love.

52. If you have no desire for filth,
Why then embrace another person,
A cage of bones that's bound by sinews
And plastered with the mud of flesh?

53. You have a lot of filth yourself—
You should be satisfied with that.
Thirsting for the unclean, you lust
For yet another sack of filth.

54. Saying "This flesh is what I like,"
You want to touch and gaze on it.
Then why don't you desire the flesh
That is devoid of conscious nature?

55. The consciousness that you desire
Cannot be touched or looked upon.
What can be is not consciousness.
Why bother with a pointless embrace?

56. Not realizing another's body
Is filth by nature is no surprise.
Not realizing that you yourself
Are filth itself is most amazing.

57. Why does your mind, addicted to filth,
Neglect the fresh, young lotus flower
Blooming beneath the cloudless sunlight
And love instead a cage of filth?

58. If you have no desire to touch
A place befouled by excrement,
Why would you want to touch the body
Out of which it originates?

59. If filth is not what you desire,
Then why do you embrace another?
The field from which they were born was filth,
As were the seeds, as was what grew them.

60. You do not want the unclean worms
Born from manure, even though they're tiny,
And yet you want what's born from filth,
A body of plentiful filth by nature.

61. Not only do you not revile
Yourself whose nature is unclean,
You want another bag of feces,
Voraciously desiring filth.

62. When you put some nice camphor and such
Or even rice and vegetables
Inside your mouth and spit it out,
The ground is dirtied and polluted.

63. If even though it's evident,
You doubt that this is so unclean,
Then look at other, fetid bodies
Discarded in the charnel grounds.

64. And when the skin is flayed from it,
You know you will be terrified,
And yet how is it you are still
Attracted to the very same thing?

65. The fragrance applied to the body
Is nothing else but sandalwood.
Why does the scent of something else
Allure you, then, to someone else?

66. Is it not best to not be attracted
To this, which naturally smells foul?
Why do the worldly, pointlessly craving,
Perfume it with nice fragrances?

67. If that sweet scent is sandalwood,
What is it here the body emits?
Why would you be attracted to someone
Because of something else's scent?

68. The body naturally has
Long hair and nails, stained whitish teeth.
It reeks, besmeared with grimy muck.
If naked, it is terrifying.

69. Why do you toil to polish up
What's like a sword that injures you?
Those crazed by efforts of self-delusion
Have set the entire earth in turmoil.

70. If seeing only skeletons
In charnel grounds repulses you,
Can you like charnel towns that teem
With animated skeletons?

71. That which is in this way unclean
Cannot be got without a cost—
Exhaustion from earning for its sake
And wounds in hells and other realms.

72. Children aren't able to earn money.
In youth, how is this happiness?
You use your life up gathering wealth.
When old, what good are your desires?

73. Some passionate but humble folk,
Exhausted by a full day's work,
Return home only to lay down
Their worn-out bodies like a corpse.

74. Others might go abroad and suffer
From weariness and long hard travel.
They wish to see their wives and children
But won't see them for a whole year.

75. Deluded by want for their own ends,
They sell themselves to help themselves.
Not gaining that, they're driven by
The winds of others' futile work.

76. Some sell their bodies and are put
To work for others, with no freedom.
The women give birth under trees
Or in the wild, wherever they can.

77. Saying they want a livelihood,
Fools who are duped by their desires
Fear for their lives but go to battle
Or enter servitude for profit.

78. Some greedy beings get themselves wounded,
While others are impaled on stakes.
There are those who are gored by spears,
And some are even burnt alive.

79. Know the travails of getting, keeping, and losing it
Make wealth a never-ending source of ill.
For those whom greed for wealth distracts, there is no chance
For freedom from the suffering of existence.

80. For the desirous, faults like these
Are plentiful, but gains are few,
Just as the oxen pulling a cart
Get only a few bites of grass.

81. For sake of paltry gains so common
That even oxen manage them,
These perfect leisures and resources,
Which are so difficult to get,
Are crushed by the ordeals of karma.

82. For just a millionth fraction of
The arduous efforts that they make
Continually for minor ends—
Pleasures that definitely perish

83. And cast them to the hells and such—
They could be buddhas, but the greedy,
Instead of awakened conduct, have
Great miseries and no awakening.

84. Considering the sufferings
Of hell and so forth, there's no weapon,
No poison, fire, abyss, or foe
That can compare to the desires.

85. Thus weary yourself of desires
And rouse delight for solitude.
Deep in a peaceful forest free
Of quarrels and disturbances,

86. On broad flat stones—delightful palaces
Cooled by the sandalwood of the moon's rays—
The fortunate pace, fanned by a woodland breeze,
Serene and silent, pondering other's weal.

87. In empty huts, by trees, or else in caves,
You may remain as long as you desire.
The pains of getting and keeping left behind,
You live without a care, dependent on none.

88. To freely act with no desires
And without ties to anyone—
Enjoyable comfort of contentment
Is hard for even a prince to find.

89. Once you've reflected on these and other
Advantages of solitude,
Then fully pacify your thoughts
And meditate on bodhichitta.

90. First meditate ardently upon
The equality of self and other.
They're equal in both pain and pleasure,
So protect everyone like yourself.

91. Although of many different kinds, the hands and so forth
Are one as a body to protect. Likewise though beings
Are different and separate in their joys and pains,
They all are equal, the same as me in wanting comfort.

92. Even though my own suffering
Does not cause harm to others' bodies,
My suffering is unbearable
Because of ego-clinging.

93. Likewise the sufferings of others
Have no effect on me, but still
Their suffering is unbearable
Because of ego-clinging.

94. I will dispel others' suffering
Since it is suffering, like my own.
I shall bring benefit to others
Since they are beings, like my body.

95. For when both I and others are
The same in wanting to be happy
And they're no different from me,
Why only work for my own pleasure?

96. And when both I and others are
The same in wanting not to suffer
And they're no different from me,
Then why protect myself, not others?

97. If I will not protect them since
Their suffering does not cause me harm,
Then future suffering as well
Does not harm me—why guard against it?

98. It is erroneous to think,
"It's me who will experience it,"
Because it is one being who dies
And yet another who is born.

99. If they whose suffering it is
Themselves must guard themselves from it,
Since the foot's pain is not the hand's,
Why should the one protect the other?

100. "Even though it's illogical,
We act from ego-clinging," you say.
We must, as much as possible,
Give up fallacious selves and others.

101. Continua and aggregates,
Like series, armies, and such, are false.
The suffering one does not exist,
So who is it that this belongs to?

102. That suffering has no owner is
No different for anyone.
I will dispel it since it's painful—
In this, why should I set a limit?

103. There's no dispute the suffering
Of everyone must be prevented.
If mine's prevented, prevent all.
Or else, like beings', not mine either.

104. "Compassion is too painful," you say,
"So why arouse it with such effort?"
But when you think of beings' torments,
How is the pain of compassion greater?

105. For if a single suffering
Eliminates many miseries,
Those with compassion will induce
That suffering in themselves and others.

106. Thus even though Supushpachandra
Knew that the king would cause him harm,
He did not shy away from pain
To end the sufferings of many.

107. Those who have trained their own mind streams
Will enter even the Incessant
With joy for quelling others' woes,
Like swans alighting on lotus ponds.

108. When beings have been liberated,
Is not the ocean of joy that brings
Sufficient in and of itself?
What good is wanting liberation?

109. So though I have done good for others,
I'm not conceited or amazed.
Solely enjoying helping others,
I've no hope for a ripened result.

110. Thus just as I protect myself
From any blame, no matter how slight,
For others, I will likewise be
Protective and compassionate.

111. Just as, due to habituation,
I know the drops of blood and semen
That came from others as myself,
Though that has no reality,

112. Why don't I similarly grasp
The bodies of other beings as me?
It also is not difficult
To see my body as someone else.

113. Knowing that I have faults while others
Are oceans of good qualities,
I'll meditate on giving up
Self-clinging while adopting others.

114. In the same way as we accept
That hands and such are body parts,
Why do we not likewise accept
The living are a part of the world?

115. The thought this selfless body is me
Arose due to habituation,
So why will the idea others
Are me not come with habituation?

116. So though I have done good for others,
I'm not conceited or amazed,
Just as there's no hope for return
When I eat my own food myself.

117. Thus just as I protect myself
From any blame, no matter how slight,
I'll cultivate compassionate,
Protective thoughts for beings.

118. That is why Avalokiteshvara
From his compassion, blessed his name
To soothe the fears that wanderers
Have even of being among people.

119. Do not turn back from difficulty—
From the power of habituation,
Though someone's name did once strike fear,
Without them, you will feel no joy.

120. All those who wish to swiftly give
Protection to themselves and others
Should practice the most excellent secret,
The exchange of self and other.

121. Due to attachment to our bodies,
We're scared by even the smallest fright.
Who wouldn't abhor this fearsome body
As if it were an enemy?

122. From the desire to cure the illness
Of hunger, thirst, and such, the body
Will make you kill birds, fish, and deer
And wait in ambush by the road.

123. And if it makes you kill your parents
Or steal what's offered the three jewels
For sake of gain or else respect
So you'll be burned in the Incessant,

124. No one who's wise would want that body,
Nor would they shield or venerate it.
Who would not look at it and see
An enemy? Who would not scorn it?

125. "If I give this, what will I enjoy?"
Such selfish thoughts are the way of fiends.
"If I enjoy this, what can I give?"
Such altruism is divine dharma.

126. If you harm others for your own sake,
You'll be tormented in hell and elsewhere.
If you are harmed for others' sake,
You will gain everything excellent.

127. Those who want high rank for themselves
Become lowly dolts in lower realms,
But those who pass it on to others
Will gain respect in the high realms.

128. If you use others for selfish ends,
You will experience servitude.
Using yourself for others' sake,
You will experience lordliness.

129. All happiness in the world is born
Of wishing others happiness.
All suffering in the world is born
Of wanting happiness for yourself.

130. What need is there to explain at length?
The childish act for their own ends;
The sages act for others' sake.
Look at the difference between them.

131. If you do not exchange your pleasures
For other beings' miseries,
You will not achieve buddhahood
Or have any happiness in samsara.

132. No need to mention the next life.
In this life, servants who don't work
And masters who do not pay wages
Will also not achieve their aims.

133. Fools throw away the perfect pleasure
Of gaining seen and unseen joys,
And, causing others misery,
They take on terrible suffering.

134. All of the violence in the world
And all the fear and suffering
Arise from clinging to a self.
What does that ogre do for me?

135. Without relinquishing your self,
You can't abandon suffering.
Just as without relinquishing fire,
You cannot avoid getting burned.

136. Therefore to calm harms to myself
And pacify others' suffering,
I'll give myself away to others
And cling to others as myself.

137. Mind, understand with certainty
That I am owned by other beings.
Now do not think of anything else
Than benefiting sentient beings.

138. It is not right to gain selfish ends
With eyes and such that others own.
It is not right to treat them badly
With eyes that are for their benefit.

139. Therefore I will put beings first.
Anything I see on my body,
I'll take away and put to use
For sake of benefiting others.

140. Make the inferior and so forth
Yourself and make yourself the other.
Then meditate without any thought
On envy, rivalry, and pride.

141. "They are respected; I am not.
I do not get as much as them.
They're praised, while I am ridiculed,
And they are happy, while I suffer.

142. "I am the one who does the work,
But they live comfortably indeed.
They're known in society as great,
While it's said I've no qualities.

143. "No qualities? What can I do?
But I have all the qualities.
There *are* some they're inferior to
And some I am superior to.

144. "My discipline, views, and so forth are
Corrupted due to the afflictions.
I've no control, so they should cure me
As best they can; I'll take the pain.

145. "But I'm not someone they would heal.
Why do they treat me with contempt?
If they're a person with qualities,
What use are their qualities to me?

146. "They've no compassion for those inside
The maws of the dread lower realms.
Conceited with external virtues,
They want to vie against the wise."

147. When I see those who are my peers,
"To make myself superior,
I'll get their things and gain respect
Even if I must fight for it.

148. "No matter what, I'll make it so
My qualities are world renowned.
I'll make sure no one ever hears
Of any of their qualities.

149. "Furthermore, I will hide my faults
So I am honored and they aren't.
Now I will easily get goods
And be respected—they will not.

150. "When they act inappropriately,
I'll watch for a long time with glee.
I will make them a laughingstock
That all revile among themselves."

151. "This wretch is trying to rival me,
It's said, but can they be my equal
In learning or intelligence,
In body, stature, or in wealth?

152. "When they hear of my qualities
That are well known to everyone,
Let them experience the rapture
Of feeling shivers of delight.

153. "Although they might possess some wealth,
We'll take it all away by force,
And if they do some work for us,
We'll give them just enough to live.

154. "We will deprive them of happiness
And always yoke them to our torments.
This one wrought miseries for us
Hundreds of times in all samsara."

155. O mind, you have spent countless aeons
Wanting to benefit yourself,
But even with such great ordeals,
You've only created suffering.

156. Therefore you must apply yourself
Completely to benefiting others.
Later you'll see the merits in this—
The Sage's words are undeceiving.

157. If you had done these acts before,
A situation such as this
That's not a buddha's perfect bliss
Would never have been possible.

158. And therefore, just as you have clung
To drops of others' sperm and blood
As being yourself, likewise you must
Meditate thus for others too.

159. You should act as a spy for others.
When you see anything on your body,
Then take away that very thing
And use it to benefit other beings.

160. "I'm comfortable; others are not.
I'm high in stature; others are low,
And I am helped, while others aren't."
Why aren't you envious of yourself?

161. Deprive yourself of happiness.
Take others' suffering on yourself.
When you think, "What is this one doing?"
Examine your own deficiencies.

162. Even the wrongs that others do
Must be transformed into your own faults.
Even the minor wrongs you do
Must be confessed to many people.

163. Proclaim especially others' fame,
So that it will outshine your own.
Employ yourself to all their ends
As if you were the lowest slave.

164. This one is rife with faults by nature,
So do not praise their fleeting virtues.
Do all you can so no one knows
Anything of their qualities.

165. In brief, for your own selfish sake,
You have caused injuries to others.
Now make it so, for beings' sake,
That all the harm will fall on you.

166. Don't let this one be impetuous
In arrogant and headstrong ways.
Instead, leave it like a new bride
Who's shy and fearful and restrained.

167. "Do that! You must remain like this!
And you must never act like that!"
Exert your power over it;
Punish it if it disobeys.

168. If, mind, you will not act like that
Even though I have told you to,
You will indeed be subjugated,
Since all wrongs are because of you.

169. The bygone days when you were able
To ruin me were different.
I see wherever you go now.
I'll destroy all your vanity.

170. Give up the idea that you still
Have purposes of your very own.
Since I have sold you off to others,
Offer your strength without despair.

171. If I get careless and do not
Deliver you to sentient beings,
It's certain you'll deliver me
Down to the keepers of the hells.

172. I've suffered long the many times
That you have given me away.
Now I remember my resentment.
I shall destroy your selfish thoughts.

173. Therefore if you want to be pleased,
Do not make pleasure for yourself.
If you want to protect yourself,
Continuously protect others.

174. The more that I protect this body,
The more it gets too tender and falls.

175. If the desires of one who's fallen
In such a way can't be fulfilled
By even this entire earth,
Who is there that can meet their wants?

176. Insatiable desires produce
Afflictions and degenerate thoughts.
Those not dependent on anything
Have never-ending excellence.

177. So don't give physical desires
An opportunity to grow.
Not clinging to anything as being
Desirable is the finest thing.

178. In the end, it will end up as ash,
Unmoving, moved by someone else.
Why do I grasp at this unclean
And frightening form as being me?

179. No matter whether it's live or dead,
What use have I of this machine?
If it's no different from a clod,
Alas, why not be rid of pride?

180. Because of doting on this body,
I've brought myself pointless miseries.
What use is getting attached or angry
For this, which is the same as wood?

181. Thus whether I take care of it,
Or vultures and the like consume it,
It feels no attachment or aversion,
So why am I attached to it?

182. If it is not itself aware
Of anger when it is disparaged
And pleasure when it is admired,
Who am I tiring myself for?

183. If you should say that someone who
Is fond of this body is my friend,
Everyone's fond of their own body,
So why am I not fond of them?

184. So I'll give up, without attachment,
This body for wanderers' benefit.
Therefore, though it has many faults,
I'll keep it, using it to act.

185. I've had enough of childish conduct.
I'll follow the footsteps of the wise.
Recalling the words on carefulness,
I'll ward off sleep and sluggishness.

186. Like the compassionate bodhisattvas,
I'll have the proper fortitude.
If I don't strive both day and night,
When will my sufferings reach an end?

187. Thus to dispel the obscurations,
I'll turn my mind from the wrong paths,
And I will rest continuously
In equipoise with the right focus.

The eighth chapter, "Teachings on Meditation," from *Entering the Way of the Bodhisattva.*

9. Transcendent Prajna

1. The Sage taught all these preparations
For the sake of prajna,
So those who wish to pacify
Suffering should develop prajna.

2. The relative and ultimate
Are stated to be the two truths.
The ultimate is not mind's sphere;
It's said that mind is relative.

3. With those, two types of people are seen,
The yogic and the ordinary.
Of these two, ordinary people
Are confuted by the yogic.

4. Due to distinctions of intellect,
Higher yogis confute the lower
By analogies that both accept,
Left unexamined for the result.

5. As worldly people think that things
Are real just as they are perceived
And not illusory, the yogis
Dispute the worldly over this.

6. It is consensus, not valid knowledge,
That there's perception of form and such.
Like the consensus the unclean
Is clean and so forth, it is false.

7. In order to introduce the worldly,
The Buddha taught that there are things.
In fact, they are not momentary.
"That contradicts the relative."

8. The yogic relative has no fault.
Compared to worldly, it's seeing suchness,
Or else the worldly could refute
Their recognizing bodies as filth.

9. The merit from illusory victors
Is like that from existent ones.
"If beings are illusory,
After they die, how are they born?"

10. Illusions will arise as long
As the conditions are assembled.
Does merely lasting a long time
Mean sentient beings truly exist?

11. Killing illusory beings and such
Are not misdeeds—they have no mind.
But merit and misdeeds arise
With those who have illusory minds.

12. Since spells and such don't have that power,
Illusory minds do not arise.
Produced by various conditions,
Illusions are various as well.

13. Nowhere is there a single condition
That's capable of everything.
"If beings still cycle relatively,
Though ultimately, they're nirvana,

14. "Then even buddhas would transmigrate—
Why bother with the way of bodhi?"
Unless the continuum of conditions
Is severed, illusions will not cease.

15. They won't arise, even relatively,
When the conditions have been severed.
"If confused mind does not exist,
What is it that observes illusions?"

16. But if for you, the illusion itself
Does not exist, then what's observed?
"In suchness, there is something else;
That image is the mind itself."

17. If mind itself is illusory,
At that time, what is seen by what?
And the Protector of the World
Has said, "Mind is not seen by mind."

18. A sword blade cannot cut itself,
And it is just the same with mind.
If you say it is like a lamp
Illuminating its own nature,

19. A lamp is not illuminated,
For it is not obscured by darkness.
"Unlike a crystal, blue does not
Depend on something else for blueness.

20. "Likewise, it's seen some things depend
On something else, and some do not."
A thing that is not blue itself
Does not itself make itself blue.

21. There is a consciousness that knows
And says a lamp is luminous,
But what is it that knows and says
That mind is luminous itself?

22. Whether it's luminous or not,
If it's not seen by anything,
Like the charms of a barren woman's daughter,
Even discussing it is pointless.

23. "If self-awareness doesn't exist,
Then how is consciousness remembered?"
When something else is experienced,
It is recalled from the connection,
Like the venom of a rat.

24. "It's seen by those with other conditions,
So it illuminates itself."
When magic eye salve is applied,
You see a vase but not the salve.

25. How things are seen or heard or known
Is not what is rebutted here.
Here it's the cause of suffering—
The thought they're true—that is refuted.

26. If you think that illusions are neither
Other than mind nor the same as it,
If real, then how are they not other?
If they're not other, it is not real.

27. What's seen—illusion—is not true,
And neither is the seer, mind.
"Samsara must have a real basis,
Otherwise it would be like space."

28. How does being based upon the real
Mean the unreal performs an action?
That mind of yours, with no companion,
Would be entirely alone.

29. When mind is free of the apprehended,
Then all become tathagatas.
In that case, what's the benefit
Of thinking there is only mind?

30. "But how does merely knowing that
All is illusion stop afflictions?
Illusionists may still feel lust
For dreamlike lovers they create."

31. Their makers have not yet abandoned
The imprints of afflictions toward
Known objects, so when they see them,
Their imprint of emptiness is weak.

32. Ingraining the imprint of emptiness
Eliminates the imprint of things.
By meditating, "Nothing exists,"
It also is abandoned later.

33. When one says "Nothing exists," the thing
That's being examined isn't observed.
Deprived of basis, how can nothing
Remain before the mind?

34. And then when neither thing nor nothing
Remains before the mind,
Because there is no other way,
There is no focus—utter peace.

35. Just as a wish-fulfilling jewel
And heaven tree fill every wish,
The kayas of the victors appear
Due to disciples and aspirations.

36. The builder of the garuda pillar
Passed away after it was blessed,
But it still neutralizes poisons
And such long after he is gone.

37. A bodhisattva, following
The way of awakening, will build
A victor's pillar and pass to
Nirvana, yet perform all deeds.

38. "How is it making offerings
To one who has no mind bears fruit?"
This has been taught to be the same,
Whether they're present or in nirvana.

39. There are results, according to scripture,
Whether they're relative or suchness,
Just as there would be a result
From a true buddha, for example.

40. "One can be freed by seeing the truths;
Why bother seeing emptiness?"
Because there's no awakening
Without this path, the scriptures teach.

41. If the Great Vehicle is not proven,
How is it that your scriptures are?
"Because they're proven to us both."
At first, they were not proven to you.

42. The reasons for believing in them
Are the same for the Great Vehicle too.
If they're true since two parties accept them,
The Vedas and such would also be true.

43. If it's because the Great Vehicle
Is in dispute, reject your own scriptures
Since they're contested by non-Buddhists,
As are some you and others challenge.

44. The teachings' root is bhikshuhood,
But bhikshuhood is difficult.
For those whose minds still have a focus,
Reaching nirvana is difficult.

45. If one is freed just by discarding
Afflictions, it's immediate.
Yet it is seen that karma has power
Over those who do not have afflictions.

46. If at that time, it's definite
That they do not have the cause, craving,
Why don't they have, just like delusion,
The unafflicted craving too?

47. Craving is due to the condition
Of feeling, and they do have feeling.
A mind that has a focus dwells
On one thing or another.

48. As with conception-free absorption,
A mind that lacks in emptiness
Might cease but will arise again,
So meditate on emptiness.

49. If you accept as the Buddha's teachings
The words included in the sutras,
Don't you accept the Great Vehicle
Is mostly the same as your sutras?

50. If all of them are flawed because
A single one is not included,
Then since one sutra is the same,
Why aren't they all the Buddha's words?

51. Just because you don't understand
The teachings Mahakashyapa
And so forth did not truly fathom,
Who says they're not to be accepted?

52. Freed from extremes of greed and fear,
To stay in samsara for the sake
Of those who suffer due to delusion
Is the result of emptiness.

53. The refutations of the position
Of emptiness are not reasonable,
So do not harbor any doubts,
And meditate on emptiness.

54. The remedy for the darkness of
The cognitive and afflictive veils
Is emptiness. Wouldn't they who want
Omniscience quickly cultivate it?

55. If fearfulness is born out of
The things that produce suffering,
Then why is it that emptiness,
The cure for suffering, provokes dread?

56. If there existed any me,
There could be fear of anything.
But since no me exists at all,
Who is there that could be afraid?

57. Teeth and hair and nails aren't me.
Bones and blood are not me either.
Mucus is not, and phlegm is not,
And neither lymph nor pus is me.

58. Fat is not me; sweat is not me;
Nor are the lungs or liver me.
Neither are the other organs.
Feces and urine are not me.

59. Muscles and skin and body heat
And breath aren't me. The orifices
Are not me, or in any way
Are the six consciousnesses either.

60. If the cognition of sound were permanent,
Sound would be apprehended at all times.
When there is nothing to be known, what knows?
And why is it described as a cognition?

61. If it is a cognition without knowing,
It follows blocks of wood are cognition too.
Thus it is certain there is no cognition
When there is nothing present to be known.

62. And if that very one knows visual form,
At that time, why does it not also hear?
If that's because there is no sound nearby,
Then there is no cognition of it either.

63. How can a nature apprehending sound
Become the apprehension of a form?
One may be thought of as both parent and child,
But that is not an actuality.

64. For in this way, the *sattva*, *rajas*, and *tamas*
Are not a child and not a parent either.
So it is not perceived to be a nature
Possessing apprehension of a sound.

65. If like an actor, that itself is seen
In different ways, then it's not permanent.
And if the different manners are just that,
Then such a oneness is unprecedented.

66. But if the different manners are not true,
Do tell me, please, what its own nature is.
"Just consciousness," you say, then in that case,
It follows that all people would be one.

67. The sentient and nonsentient would be one
As well, since their existence is the same.
When the particulars are also false,
What basis is there for similarity?

68. Nor can what is nonsentient be the self,
Because it has no mind, like jugs and such.
But if it knows from being conjoined with mind,
It follows the nonsentient perishes.

69. If there is no change in the self,
What does cognition do for it?
In this way, you have made unknowing
And inert space into the self.

70. "With no self, the relationship
Of act and result would make no sense.
One perishes when the act is done,
So whose act would it be?" you ask.

71. It's proven to us both the bases
Of act and result are separate
And that the self does not act on them.
Is this not pointless to debate?

72. It cannot possibly be seen
That one with the cause would have the result.
The actor and the reaper are taught
Based on a single continuum.

73. The past and future minds are not
A me, since they do not exist.
If the arisen mind is me,
When it is gone, the me is no longer.

74. Just as when one dissects the trunk
Of a banana tree, there's nothing,
When scrutinized analytically,
The me as well is nothing true.

75. "If sentient beings do not exist,
For whom should one arouse compassion?"
For those projected by delusion,
Whom we accept for the sake of results.

76. "Whose is the fruit if there are no beings?"
That's true; the wish is from delusion.
For the sake of quelling suffering,
Don't block delusion about the result.

77. Delusions of a self increase
The cause of suffering—the ego.
"But there's no stopping that," you say.
To cultivate selflessness is supreme.

78. The body's not the feet or calves,
Nor are the thighs or hips the body.
It's not the belly or the back;
Neither is it the chest or arms.

79. It's not the ribs, hands, armpits, shoulders,
And it is not the organs either.
The head and throat are not the body,
So what, then, is the body here?

80. Now if the body were to dwell
Partially in all of them,
Its parts would thus dwell in those parts,
But where would it reside itself?

81. If the entirety of the body
Should dwell within the hands and such,
Then there would be as many bodies
As there are hands, et cetera.

82. If there's no body, outside or in,
How's there a body in hands and such?
If it's not separate from the hands
And such, then how does it exist?

83. Thus there's no body. From delusion,
We think of hands and such as the body,
Just like perceiving a scarecrow as
A human from its specific shape.

84. While the conditions are assembled,
The body will appear as human.
Likewise as long as there are hands
And such, they'll seem to be a body.

85. In the same way, what are the hands,
Which are assemblages of fingers?
Those are assemblages of knuckles.
Dissecting knuckles into their parts,

86. The parts, too, divide into atoms.
Dividing atoms into sides,
Those, too, can split and have, like space,
No parts, so there are no atoms either.

87. In this way, what discerning person
Would lust for such a dreamlike form?
When in this way there is no body,
What is a man? What is a woman?

88. If pain exists in suchness, then
Why does it not distress the cheerful?
Why don't those wracked with grief enjoy
The tasty, if it's pleasurable?

89. If it is not experienced
Because the stronger overwhelms it,
Then how can something that in nature
Is not experience be a feeling?

90. "The pain is there in a subtle form."
Has its gross form not been dispelled?
If it's a different, mere pleasure,
The subtle form would be of that.

91. If causes of its contrary
Arise, so pain does not occur,
Does that not prove that to conceive
Of it as feeling is just fixation?

92. So therefore, as its antidote,
Cultivate this investigation.
The dhyana that grows in the field
Of analysis is food for yogis.

93. If there's a gap between the object
And faculty, where is the contact?
If there's no gap, they would be one,
And what would be in contact with what?

94. An atom can't penetrate an atom;
There is no space and they are equal.
They won't merge without penetration,
And without merging, there's no contact.

95. How is it logical to say
That there is contact with the partless?
If you should happen to observe
The partless come in contact, show me.

96. It's most illogical to contact
An immaterial consciousness,
Or, as examined earlier,
Assemblies, as they are not things.

97. If contact thus does not exist,
Then out of what does feeling arise?
For sake of what are these travails?
What causes injury to whom?

98. If there's not anyone who feels
And there's not any feeling either,
Once we have seen this situation,
Why is it craving would not cease?

99. When seeing or touching, it's by a nature
That's dreamlike and illusory.
As they arise together with mind,
Feelings are not perceived by it.

100. The earlier would be remembered
But not experienced by a later.
They're not experienced by themselves,
Nor are they felt by something else.

101. There is no one at all who feels,
And feelings therefore are not real.
Thus in this egoless assemblage,
How then can they cause any harm?

102. Mind does not dwell in faculties,
In form and such, or in between.
Mind is not inside and not outside,
And there is nowhere else it's found.

103. What's not a body and not other,
Not mingled and not separate,
Is nothing at all, and for this reason,
The nature of beings is nirvana.

104. If mind precedes that which is known,
What does it focus on to arise?
If mind and the known are synchronous,
What does it focus on to arise?

105. If it is after what is known,
What does the mind arise from then?
In such a way, one cannot realize
The arising of any phenomenon.

106. "If there is thus no relative,
Then how is it there are two truths?
If it's from another relative,
Then how could beings reach nirvana?"

107. But that is someone else's thought;
It is not their own relative.
It would exist if recognized later;
If not, there is no relative.

108. The thought and what is thought of both
Are each dependent on the other.
All the analyses are stated
According to the common consensus.

109. "If the analysis must be
Analyzed analytically,
So too must that analysis
Be analyzed, ad infinitum."

110. When the object has been analyzed,
There is no basis to analyze.
Without a base, it won't arise,
And this is what is called *nirvana*.

111. For those to whom these two seem true,
This is extremely difficult.
If entities are proven by knowing,
What basis does knowing have to exist?

112. But if what's known proves there is knowing,
What basis has what's known for being?
If each exists by force of the other,
Then neither of them could exist.

113. One's not a parent without a child,
So how then can the child arise?
Without a child, there is no parent.
Likewise these two are nonexistent.

114. "A shoot arises from a seed,
And due to this, the seed is known.
Why don't we know the object exists
Through the cognition it produces?"

115. A mind that's other than the shoot
Realizes that there was a seed.
How is it known that there exists
A knower by which the known is realized?

116. First, the people of the world
Can see perceptually all causes.
Distinctions of lotus stalks and such
Are born of distinctions in the causes.

117. "What makes distinctions in the causes?"
Distinctions in preceding causes.
"Why can a cause produce a result?"
It's from the previous cause's power.

118. If God is the cause of sentient beings,
Then tell us first, please, what is God?
"The elements," you say. So be it—
Why bother over a mere name?

119. But earth and such are multiple,
Impermanent, inanimate,
And not divine. They're stepped upon
And filthy, so they are not God.

120. Space is not God, since it's inert.
The self is not; it's been refuted.
An inconceivable creator
Is beyond thought; why speak of it?

121. What do you posit He creates?
A self? Aren't that and earth and such
And God by nature permanent?
Cognition arises from its object

122. Without beginning; pleasure and pain,
From actions. Do say what He creates.
And if the cause has no beginning,
How's there a beginning to results?

123. Why is He not creating always?
He's not dependent on something else.
There's nothing else He did not make,
So what could He depend upon?

124. If He's dependent, the assembly
Would be the cause, and God would not.
When they're assembled, He would have
No power to not create, and when
They're not, no power to create.

125. If God creates without the wish to do so,
It follows He's controlled by something else.
And if He wants to, He depends on that.
Even creating, how is He almighty?

126. Those who say atoms are permanent
Have been refuted earlier.
The permanent, primal substance is
The cause of beings, hold the Samkhyas.

127. They say that when the qualities—
The so-called sattva, rajas, and tamas—
Are balanced, that's the primal substance.
Unbalanced, they are called the world.

128. For one to have three natures is
Illogical, so it's nonexistent.
Likewise the qualities don't exist,
For each of them is triple too.

129. It is far-fetched for sound and such
To exist without the qualities,
And pleasure and such aren't possible
In cloth and other mindless things.

130. If the nature of their cause is things,
Haven't we analyzed things already?
For you, the cause is pleasure and such,
But blankets don't arise from them.

131. Pleasure and so forth come from blankets;
Without them, there's no pleasure and such.
And pleasure and so forth as well
Are never observed as permanent.

132. If instances of pleasure exist,
Why isn't the feeling apprehended?
You say just that has become subtle,
But how can it be gross and subtle?

133. If they lose grossness and turn subtle,
Then gross or subtle, they are transient.
Why do you not assert all things
Are similarly impermanent?

134. If grossness is not other than pleasure,
Pleasure is clearly impermanent.
If you say something nonexistent
Cannot arise—it doesn't exist—

135. A nonexistent instance arising
Amounts to this, despite your wish.
If the result dwells in the cause,
Then eating food is eating feces,

136. And for the price of cotton cloth,
You should buy cotton seeds and wear them.
"Since they're deluded, people don't see it."
But those who know reality

137. Present this, and there are some people
Who know it—why do they not see it?
If worldly folk lack valid knowledge,
Then seeing the manifest is not true.

138. "If valid cognition were invalid,
Then would not what is known be false?
Therefore, in suchness, meditating
On emptiness is illogical."

139. Sans contact with imagined things,
Their nothingness is not apprehended.
Therefore the unreality
Of a false thing is clearly false.

140. Thus when a child dies in a dream,
The thought that they do not exist
Negates the thought they do exist,
And yet, it also is a fiction.

141. Having investigated thus,
Nothing without a cause exists,
And nothing dwells in the conditions,
Individually or combined.

142. It does not come from somewhere else,
Nor does it stay, nor does it go.
Though the deluded say it's true,
How does it differ from illusion?

143. What an illusion emanates
And that which causes emanate:
Scrutinize where it is they come from
And also where it is they go.

144. That which is seen when something else
Is present but not when it's absent
Is fabricated, like a reflection.
How is there any truth to it?

145. How would a cause be necessary
For a thing that exists already?
However, if it doesn't exist,
How would a cause be necessary?

146. Even a thousand million causes
Cannot transform the nonexistent.
How in that phase is it a thing?
And what else would become a thing?

147. If at the time of nonexistence,
A thing can't possibly exist,
When can a thing come into being?
And if a thing has not arisen,
That nonexistence does not vanish.

148. Without removing nonexistence,
There's no chance for the thing to be.
Nor can a thing become nonexistent—
For it would therefore have two natures.

149. In this way, there is no cessation,
Nor is there any existent thing.
Thus at all times, all wanderers
Have not been born and do not cease.

150. Wandering beings are like dreams,
Like a banana tree when probed.
Reaching nirvana and not reaching
Are not, in suchness, any different.

151. With things, which in this way are empty,
What's there to get? What's there to lose?
And who is there to be respected
Or denigrated, and by whom?

152. Whence do pleasure and suffering come?
What's to dislike and what's to like?
When you investigate, in suchness,
Who's there that craves? What's there to crave?

153. When it's examined, in this world
Of living beings, who here dies?
What will become? What once became?
And what are family and friends?

154. All those like me must understand
That everything is just like space.
The causes, strife and merriment,
Make those who want pleasure for themselves

155. Become enraged or else exultant.
They grieve, they toil, and they dispute.
They slash and stab each other, doing
Misdeeds that make their lives arduous.

156. Returning, returning to higher realms,
Consuming, consuming the many pleasures,
They die and plunge to lower realms—
Intense, long-lasting agonies.

157. So many abysses in existence!
And there, such things as these aren't suchness.
There, too, they're incompatible.
In existence, there is no such suchness.

158. There, the incomparable and dreadful
Oceans of suffering are endless.
And there, one has so little strength;
And there, life is so very short.

159. There, in maintaining life and health,
In weariness from hunger and thirst,
In sleep and in adversity,
In the fruitless company of fools,

160. Life passes quickly, pointlessly.
Discernment is so hard to find.
And there, what method could there be
To stop the habits of distraction?

161. There, too, the maras try to make
One fall into great lower realms.
And there, wrong paths are plentiful.
It's difficult to get past doubt.

162. It's hard to find these leisures again;
Most hard to find a buddha appearing.
Hard to give up the flood of afflictions.
Alas! The stream of suffering!

163. Although the suffering is extreme,
They do not see their own misery.
Alas! It is most fitting to grieve
For those deluged by suffering!

164. Just as some bathe repeatedly
But enter flames again and again,
Although they suffer terribly,
They have the conceit that they are happy.

165. Likewise they live with the pretense
That they will never grow old or die.
But first they're slain, and then there comes
The terrible fall to lower realms.

166. So when will I bring peace to those
Ravaged by fires of suffering
By showering down from clouds of merit
A rain of comforts to sustain them?

167. And when will I, free of all focus,
Respectfully accumulate merit
And then teach emptiness to those
Whose focus brings them ruin?

———————

The ninth chapter, "Transcendent Prajna," from *Entering the Way of the Bodhisattva*.

10. DEDICATION

1. By the merit of my having written
The *Way of the Bodhisattva*,
May every wandering being enter
The bodhisattvas' ways.

2. May everyone in all directions
Who's anguished or diseased
In body or mind gain, through my merit,
An ocean of happiness.

3. As long as they are in samsara,
May their happiness never wane.
May beings continuously obtain
The bodhisattvas' joy.

4. May all the beings in the hells,
As many as there are
In every universe, delight
In the joys of the Blissful Realm.

5. May all those stricken by cold find warmth;
Those stricken by heat be cooled
By boundless oceans of waters born
From great clouds of bodhisattvas.

6. May sword-leaf forests become for them
Thick groves of sandalwood.
May the trunks of *shalmali* trees grow
Into wish-fulfilling trees.

7. May the regions of the hells become delightful
With lakes of aromatic lotuses
Made beautiful by gray geese, ducks, ruddy geese,
White swans, and so forth, calling pleasantly.

8. May the heaps of embers become mounds of jewels;
The burning ground become a crystal floor.
May the crushing mountains also become temples
Of worship that are filled with sugatas.

9. From today onward, may the rains of lava,
Embers, and armaments be a rain of flowers.
May those who strike each other with their weapons
From now on playfully toss flowers instead.

10. May those sunk in the Unfordable River—whose water is
like fire—
Their flesh all fallen off, their bones as white as jasmine flowers,
By the power of my virtue achieve the body of a god
And dwell in goddesses' company by the Mandakini.

11. "What frightens so the terrible henchmen of the Lord of
Death, the crows, and vultures?
Whose might," they wonder, "this fine power dispelling the
gloom all round and bringing us joy?"
Looking up, may they see Vajrapani blazing in the center of
the sky.
Freed of misdeeds by the power of utter joy, may they consort
with him.

12. Seeing a rain of blossoms mixed with scented water
Drench and extinguish the infernal conflagrations,
May the beings in hell be sated with a sudden pleasure,
And wondering why that is, behold there Padmapani.

13. "Friends, cast away your fear and hurry here! Who could
this be, now come to us
Relieving all our suffering, exuding the energy of joy,
Protecting beings from all, the bodhisattva who has roused
compassion,
The youth with hair in a topknot who dispels our every fear?

14. "Behold! See how a hundred gods revere his lotus feet with
their tiaras.
His eyes are moist with compassion; a shower of many flowers
falls upon his head.
Look at this lovely palace where a thousand goddesses praise
him in song!"
May the denizens of hell let forth such a clamor when they
behold Manjughosha.

15. Then through my virtue, may the beings in the hells,
Seeing a cloud of bodhisattvas free of obscurations
Led by Samantabhadra shower down on them
A comforting, cool, fragrant rain, take true delight.

16. May animals' fear of being eaten
By one another vanish.
Like humans in Unpleasant Sound,
May hungry ghosts be happy.

17. May streams of milk flowing from the hands
Of noble Lokeshvara
Ever satiate, bathe, and refresh
The *preta* hungry ghosts.

18. May everyone who's blind now see,
And may the deaf always hear.
May the pregnant give birth without pain,
Just like Queen Mayadevi.

19. May those who are naked obtain clothing;
The hungry acquire food.
May those who are thirsty procure water
And delicious beverages.

20. May beggars gain prosperity;
Those wracked with grief gain joy.
May the despondent be relieved
And have great stability.

21. May every being who is sick
Be swiftly cured of illness.
May none of wanderers' maladies
Ever occur again.

22. May those who are frightened have no fears;
May all in bonds be freed.
May the powerless be powerful
And friendly with each other.

23. May all directions be propitious
For every traveler.
May they accomplish without effort
The aims for which they travel.

24. May those embarked on boats and ships
Accomplish their intentions,
And may they safely reach the shore
To rejoice with their families.

25. May those astray on desolate paths
Meet travelers and journey
Unafraid of bandits, tigers, and such,
With ease and unfatigued.

26. May the young and old without protection
In wretched, roadless wilds—
Asleep, inebriated, or mad—
Be guarded by the gods.

27. Freed of all lack of leisure, may they
Have faith, compassion, and prajna.
May they, with perfect food and conduct,
Recall their past lives always.

28. May all have wealth as endless as
The treasury of the sky,
Enjoying it as they wish without
Any quarreling or threats.

29. May beings with little vitality
Be vigorous and robust.
May those ascetics with bad physiques
Have the most sublime bodies.

30. May all the women in the world
Gain favorable positions.
May those who are lowly gain high status
And also vanquish pride.

31. May every being without exception,
Through this merit of mine,
Abandon all misdeeds and then
Act virtuously always.

32. Never parted from bodhichitta, may they
Engage in enlightened conduct.
May they be accepted by the buddhas
And give up the acts of maras.

33. May every sentient being have
Immeasurably long life.
May all live happily forever.
May the word *death* be unheard.

34. May pleasure groves of wishing trees
Filled with dharma proclaimed
By buddhas and the buddhas' offspring
Abound in all directions.

35. Everywhere may the ground be free
Of gravel, and so forth,
As even as a palm, as smooth
As *vaidurya* in nature.

36. May great assemblies of bodhisattvas
Be seated all around,
And may they beautify the earth
With their magnificence.

37. May all corporeal beings hear
The unceasing sound of dharma
From every bird, tree, and light ray,
And even from the sky.

38. May they perpetually encounter
The buddhas and their children
And with boundless clouds of offerings,
Revere the teacher of beings.

39. May the gods make the rains fall in season.
May crops be excellent.
May monarchs act according to dharma,
And may the people thrive.

40. May medicines be efficacious
And mantras be accomplished.
May dakinis and rakshasas
And such be compassionate.

41. May no sentient being be miserable,
None wicked, none diseased.
May none be fearful or despised.
Let no one be unhappy.

42. Thriving with reading and recitation,
May temples be well established.
May the sangha—always harmonious—
Accomplish its purposes.

43. May bhikshus with the wish to train
Find solitary places,
Give up all distraction, and meditate
With minds that are workable.

44. May the bhikshunis be supported
And give up quarrels and harm.
May everyone who has gone forth
Have unbroken discipline.

45. May those who've broken vows repent,
And always giving up wrong,
Be born in the higher realms and keep
Their vows inviolate.

46. May panditas be venerated
And also receive alms.
Their mind streams pure, may they be known
In every direction.

47. Without enduring the lower realms' pains
Or undergoing hardship,
With a body better than a god's,
May beings soon become buddhas.

48. May every being frequently make
Offerings to all buddhas.
May they be happy always with
The buddhas' infinite bliss.

49. The bodhisattvas' wishes for
The sake of beings fulfilled,
May sentient beings easily gain
What the protectors intend.

50. Likewise may the pratyekabuddhas
And shravakas be happy.

51. Until through Manjughosha's kindness,
I achieve the level Joyous,
Always may I recall my lives,
Go forth, and be ordained.

52. Even with meager fare, may I
Live with vitality.
In all my lives, may I find places
Of perfect solitude.

53. Whenever I have the wish to see him
Or ask of him a question,
May I see without impediment
Manjushri, the protector.

54. Just as Manjushri acts to achieve
The benefit of all beings
To the ends of space in the ten directions,
May my deeds be the same.

55. For as long as space endures,
As long as there are beings,
I will remain to eliminate
The sufferings of beings.

56. Whatever the sufferings of wanderers,
May they all ripen on me.
May the sangha of bodhisattvas bring
Beings to happiness.

57. Sole cure for beings' suffering,
Source of all happiness,
May the teachings remain for a long time,
Supported and respected.

58. I bow to Manjushri, through whose kindness
A virtuous mind arose.
I also bow to the spiritual friends
Whose kindness made me thrive.

The tenth chapter, "Dedication," from *Entering the Way of the Bodhisattva*. This completes *Entering the Way of the Bodhisattva* by Master Shantideva.

The Tibetan translation was reviewed and finalized by the Indian master Sarvajnadeva and the great editor-translator Bande Paltsek according to a manuscript from Kashmir. Later, the Indian master Dharma Shri Bhadra and the editor-translators Bande Rinchen Sangpo and Shakya Lodrö revised, retranslated, and edited it according to a manuscript from central India. At a later time, the Indian master Sumatikirti and the editor-translator bhikshu Loden Sherap corrected it again and finalized it.

Translated into English from the canonical Tibetan text in comparison with the extant Sanskrit by the bhikshu Karma Lodrö Choephel.

A CONTEMPORARY GUIDE TO THE
WAY OF THE BODHISATTVA

Khenpo David Karma Choephel

In a skeptical time
when tales of wonders
no longer resonate,
what greater miracle
is there than simple,
direct words
that instill faith
and inspire action?
I bow in gratitude.

But the strangeness of centuries,
of mores removed from,
remote to,
this
materialist
age

might silt the flow
of the sweet
nectar of your words
and slow
their workings,

so I shall try
to let them
run
freely.

INTRODUCTION

SINCE THE EXTRAORDINARY day when Shantideva recited it before a large crowd at the ancient Buddhist university of Nalanda, *Entering the Way of the Bodhisattva* has been recognized as one of the most important works of Mahayana Buddhism. In its original Sanskrit, its fame spread throughout northern India and into Southeast Asia, and the Tibetan translation became one of the foundational texts of study and practice for all schools of Tibetan Buddhism. It is revered not only for its presentation of practical advice for developing bodhichitta and its clear explanation of Middle Way philosophy but also for its memorable verse and inspiring imagery. On a purely literary level, the *Way of the Bodhisattva* ranks among the great long poems of world literature, the meditation of an individual struggling to live up to a lofty ideal. Ranging in tone from pathos and disgust with the narrator's own failings to exultant hope, Shantideva's verses are always imbued with deep compassion, even when he uses sarcasm or humor. For Buddhist readers, it presents a clear description of how to rouse bodhichitta, incorporate its practice into all aspects of our lives, and progress down the path to buddhahood. For non-Buddhists, it gives helpful advice on how to become a better, more compassionate person.

However, the text presents some difficulties for modern readers. It was written more than thirteen hundred years ago by a monk at one of the greatest universities of ancient India for an audience that was primarily male, monastic, and well-versed in Buddhist thought. Not only is it peppered with allusions obscure to a twenty-first-century audience but its underlying assumptions are different from those of the twenty-first century, and readers may not be familiar with the issues that Shantideva addresses. This guide to the *Way of the Bodhisattva* is intended to summarize its general thought, provide background information, and explain unfamiliar terms and allusions in order to serve as a bridge between Shantideva's traditional Mahayana Buddhist ideas and contemporary English readers. Passages that are difficult to understand on their own or that address significant points of Buddhist thought are given the most attention, but without going into detail.[1] My explanations are based primarily upon the commentary by Pawo Tsuglak Trengwa, a sixteenth-century master of the Karma Kagyu school,[2] with some references to the other Indian and Tibetan commentaries.

The *Way of the Bodhisattva* is considered an important text of Mahayana Buddhist thought. Though Buddhism originated in the sixth century BCE, the Mahayana did not appear until several centuries later. Instead, what flourished at first were the teachings of the Foundation vehicle,[3] which are (as the English term implies) the foundation for all the subsequent developments in Buddhist thought. They teach that sentient beings take an infinite number of rebirths in the beginningless cycle of existence called "samsara." Some of those rebirths are in higher realms such as the human realm, but most often beings are born in the lower realms of the hells, hungry ghosts, and animals, where the suffering is intolerable. Even the pleasures of the higher realms are temporary and change, leading to further suffering. The Buddha taught that this all happens because of karmic cause and effect: motivated by mistaken self-interest and ego-clinging, sentient beings are impelled by defiled mind-states to act in ways that lead to rebirth and perpetuate the cycle of suffering. According to the Foundation vehicle, the method to break this cycle is to meditate on the four noble truths and follow the noble eightfold path. This leads the meditators to see the nature of the truth, which frees them from ego-clinging and brings them to achieve liberation from samsara. In this manner, the Foundation vehicle emphasizes practices that lead to realizing one's own selfless nature and finding liberation. Historically, there were several Foundation vehicle schools, but the only one remaining is the Theravada, which thrives in Sri Lanka, Thailand, Burma, and other areas of Southeast Asia, as well as in Western countries.

Mahayana Buddhism began to spread widely some several hundred years after the Buddha passed away, perhaps in the first or second century BCE. By the second century CE, it was flourishing in India. It spread into modern-day Afghanistan and Pakistan, along the Silk Road into China, and from there into Japan, Korea, and Vietnam. It spread separately into Tibet from the eighth century. Mahayana Buddhists accept all of the tenets of the Foundation vehicle, but for them, liberating themselves alone and leaving all other sentient beings behind in samsara is not enough. They reason that if our own suffering is so unbearable that we must achieve liberation, then others' suffering is equally unbearable and must also be relieved. Thus the main difference between the Foundation vehicle and the Mahayana is the motivation: whether to seek liberation for oneself alone or to develop the ability to also guide other sentient beings to liberation, just as the Buddha did. Because the goal of the Mahayana is vaster, it emphasizes developing boundless, unbiased compassion and teaches more profound meditations that lead to seeing not only the lack of an individual self but also the interdependent nature of all phenomena. Within the Mahayana, there are several different schools; Shantideva belongs to the Middle Way, or Madhyamaka, which is often considered to have the most profound view. Still, the foundational teachings of rebirth, karmic cause and effect, and the possibility of liberation form the basis of Shantideva's teachings and are integral to his reasoning.

SHANTIDEVA AND HIS WORK

Traditional commentaries on texts such as the *Way of the Bodhisattva* usually open with a brief account of the life of the author in order to inspire faith in them and their work. But these life stories often present a problem for modern readers. Ancient Indian sources rarely recorded or paid much attention to the types of details considered important by contemporary scholars and readers, while the stories of experiences, visions, and miracles that feature in so many life stories do not seem credible to many modern people. This problem is especially acute for Shantideva's life, with its paucity of documentation and plethora of wonders.

It is thought that Shantideva lived in the late seventh or early eighth century. Among the various accounts of his life, the most commonly told version is the "seven wondrous tales." It relates how he was born as a prince and known by the name Shantivarman. When he was young, he meditated upon the bodhisattva Manjushri, who embodies the prajna (the ability to discern what is from what is not) of all the buddhas, and had many visions of the bodhisattva. The night before he was to be crowned king, Manjushri appeared to him and told him it would not be right for him to sit on the throne, so he fled the palace and went forth to become a monk. He was ordained and given the name Shantideva.

Shantideva then came to the great Buddhist university of Nalanda, which at that time had several thousand students. Because of the strength of his meditation on Manjushri, he did not need to study, even though everyone else at Nalanda did so intensively. The other monks criticized him for his apparent laziness and nicknamed him Bhusuku, or "eat, sleep, poop," for that is all they thought he ever did. As a ruse to get him to leave Nalanda in embarrassment, they arranged that he should be given the "honor" of teaching from a high lion throne. He agreed, and a large assembly (likely consisting primarily of monks) gathered to hear him teach, or perhaps to watch the spectacle of his failure. He somehow managed to get onto the throne without anyone seeing him climb onto it and then surprised the audience by asking them whether he should teach something they had already heard or something new. They asked him to recite something new, and he recited the *Way of the Bodhisattva* from start to finish. When he came to verse 34 in the ninth chapter, "And then when neither thing nor nothing," he levitated higher and higher into the sky, eventually disappearing, yet his voice continued teaching the remainder of the work.

Through their meditation, many of the scholars in the audience had developed the ability to remember something after hearing or seeing it just once, and they compiled the text from memory. The scholars from Kashmir came up with a seven-hundred-stanza version in nine chapters, whereas the scholars from Magadha in central India compiled a one-thousand-stanza version in ten chapters.[4] Unable to agree as to which was the correct version, they sent a search party to find Shantideva, who confirmed that the ten-chapter version was correct and also told them where to find his other works, the *Compendium of the Sutras* and the *Compendium of the Trainings*, in his cell in Nalanda.[5]

Relatively soon after it was taught, the *Way of the Bodhisattva* became quite popular, spreading throughout India and beyond, even into Indonesia.[6] It is said that there were 108 commentaries on it written in Sanskrit, though only ten survive, mostly in Tibetan translation.[7] Within a century of its composition, it was included among the first Buddhist texts translated into Tibetan, likely around the turn of the ninth century. This translation, done by the great early translator Bande Kawa Paltsek and the Indian master Sarvajnadeva, was of the Kashmiri seven-hundred-stanza version. Later, the translators Rinchen Sangpo (958–1055) and Shakya Lodrö, together with the Indian pandita Dharma Shri Bhadra, revised the earlier translation and updated it to match a manuscript from Magadha of the thousand-stanza version. Finally, Ngok Lotsawa Loden Sherap (1059–1109) and the Indian master Sumatikirti revised the translation for a second time, producing the final, canonical version of the Tibetan text.

Today, there are several versions of the text. There are numerous differences among the many editions of the canonical Tibetan text, mostly minor but a few significant. There is also a Tibetan manuscript, most likely of the original translation in seven hundred verses, which was found in the Dunhuang caves in Gansu Province, China, as well as a Sanskrit edition based on manuscripts found in Nepal. The Sanskrit and the canonical Tibetan are quite similar, but some words and lines are different, and entire stanzas found in one are missing in the other. This suggests that the canonical Tibetan was translated from a different version of the Sanskrit than what is extant today. With so many versions, it is quite natural to wonder which is the most authoritative.

For Western academics, the most common approach is to analyze and compare the different versions of the text, both Tibetan and Sanskrit, to determine what might have been the actual, original words of the author.[8] In contrast, the traditional Tibetan approach finds authority in lineage. A text is considered authentic if it has been transmitted in an unbroken lineage of masters teaching disciples, who teach their disciples in turn. The canonical Tibetan version of the *Way of the Bodhisattva* is grounded in such a tradition that can be traced back to the Indian masters who taught these texts to Tibetans, and even to Shantideva himself.[9] Both the Tibetan and Western approaches have their own strengths and weaknesses. The former is a time-tested, living tradition of actually practicing the teachings, but it has the danger of being too credulous. The latter provides methods and materials that help to evaluate the different versions of the text, but it also has the danger of being overly critical of material that may actually be authentic. Though a deeper inquiry into this issue would be interesting, for the sake of brevity, I will not delve into it here.

1. Benefits: The Inspiration for Bodhichitta

T HE TITLE OF Shantideva's text tells us quite a bit about his intent in writing it. The canonical version gives the Sanskrit title as *Bodhisatvacarya avatāra*.[1] *Bodhisattva* means a being who has developed the genuine, uncontrived resolve to achieve buddhahood for the sake of all other sentient beings and has made a vow to do so. *Carya* (pronounced "charya") means "conduct" or "way"—what someone must do to take and keep the bodhisattva vow. *Avatāra* can be translated as "entering," which means that this work introduces the ways of a bodhisattva in a manner that is appropriate for beginners to practice. The full title of the work in English is therefore *Entering the Way of the Bodhisattva*, though the word *entering* is often dropped for convenience. Thus the title tells us that the work gives an introduction to the practice of a bodhisattva—rousing bodhichitta, taking the bodhisattva vow, and keeping that vow by practicing the path.

Shantideva teaches this practice over ten chapters. The first three describe how to rouse bodhichitta and take the bodhisattva vow, and the final seven teach the methods to keep that vow and practice the path of a bodhisattva. Among the first three chapters, the first describes the great benefits of bodhichitta in order to inspire us to take the bodhisattva vow, and then the second and third together describe how to actually take the vow. But before beginning the main portion of the text, Shantideva begins with three opening verses that, following tradition, pay homage to the buddhas, set forth his intention in writing the work, and express his humility.

The fourth and fifth stanzas then describe the necessary conditions for practicing the path of a bodhisattva.

THE OPENING VERSES

The canonical text includes two homages, but the first of these—the homage to the buddhas and bodhisattvas—is not Shantideva's. Instead, it was added by the Tibetan translators, following a custom of beginning a translation with a homage in order to ensure that it would be successfully completed.

Shantideva's work itself begins with a three-line homage[2] to the three jewels—the buddhas, dharma, and sangha (verse 1), who are called "jewels" because they are as rare and supremely precious as the wish-fulfilling jewels of Indian lore. He first pays homage to the buddhas—beings who started out as ordinary people such as ourselves but were able, through the power of their contemplation and meditation, to truly realize the nature of things and awaken to complete enlightenment. Traditionally, the buddhas are called by several different names, each of which speaks to a different quality. The word *buddha*, Sanskrit for "awakened," means that they have awakened from the sleep of ignorance. They are called *victors* because they have been victorious in the struggle over the four maras, demons who personify the different types of clinging that must be overcome to achieve enlightenment. Another word is *tathagata*, which means someone who has gone to or realized (*gata*) suchness (*tatha*), the nature of things. Buddhas are also called *sages*, a common translation of the Sanskrit word *muni*, which is explained as meaning "silenced," because they have stilled all the negativities of their body, speech, and mind. In this verse, the buddhas are called by the Sanskrit word *sugatas*. The prefix *su-* means "excellently," and *gata* (as above) means "gone" or "realized"—a buddha has transcended ordinary existence and reached the final, perfect result of buddhahood, never to regress. Sugatas is in the plural because the historical Buddha Shakyamuni is said to be just one of an infinite number of buddhas who have appeared in the past or will appear in the future in any of the countless worlds that Buddhism teaches exist. Here, Shantideva prostrates to all of them, who are the first of the three jewels.

What distinguishes buddhas from ordinary sentient beings is that they have the qualities of complete and perfect wisdom, love, and power, which are referred to in the second line as the *dharmakaya* or "body of qualities." By mentioning this in the homage, Shantideva is pointing out that we should view the buddhas not as ordinary, perishable flesh and blood but as luminous wisdom that sees the ultimate nature. But *dharmakaya* can also be taken to mean the dharma, the second of the three jewels. The word *dharma* often refers to the teachings of Buddhism, but what it actually means is the realization of those great beings who have seen the nature of the truth and the way that they express it in words. The dharmakaya of the Buddha is the ultimate manifestation of this.

Shantideva also pays homage to the bodhisattvas, who are called the offspring of the buddhas in the verse because they are born from the buddhas' teachings and uphold the buddhas' lineage, much as children uphold their parents' family line. The bodhisattvas represent the third of the three jewels, the sangha (the community of Buddhist practitioners who have realized the ultimate nature). In this way, Shantideva pays homage to all three jewels—the buddha, dharma, and sangha—as well as to his abbots, teachers, parents, and anyone else who deserves respect.

The last two lines of the first stanza are the pledge to compose the treatise. Most traditional Buddhist works open with a pledge to compose because making a firm commitment at the outset gives the author a greater impetus to actually complete the work—to leave it unfinished would be to break a promise. This pledge also indicates Shantideva's intention to draw on the teachings in Buddhist scripture to teach his main topic, how to take and keep the bodhisattva vow to bring all sentient beings to buddhahood. Taking and keeping the bodhisattva vow is not a light matter, for the attitude of a bodhisattva is diametrically opposed to our habitual patterns of ego-clinging and self-protection, and training oneself in it takes a great deal of effort. For this reason, Shantideva gives us instructions on how to rouse bodhichitta and take the vow, how to keep the vow, and how to restore it if we slip. If we follow these steps, we will achieve buddhahood and bring great benefit to ourselves and others. Thus his pledge to write the work also implicitly teaches his reasons for writing it.

In verses 2 and 3, Shantideva expresses his humility while downplaying his abilities and the scope of his intentions. From a modern perspective, it might seem as if he is undercutting himself, but traditionally such modesty is considered an important antidote to pride. Furthermore, it is also sometimes said that the more someone learns about the dharma, the more they realize how much they do not know. A genuine expression of humility thus becomes a sign of the author's qualities. Implicitly, Shantideva is providing an example of how bodhisattvas should be modest and humble even as they have strong confidence in themselves.

The next two stanzas (verses 4–5) describe how rare it is to have all the conditions necessary for practicing the dharma and how they must be put to good use while we have them. There are two conditions we must have: the precious human body and the faith and determination to use it to practice dharma.

For Shantideva and his audience (as for all traditional Buddhists), sentient beings have cycled from beginningless time through various rebirths due to their actions—their karma. Their virtuous actions lead to rebirth in the higher realms of humans, gods, and demigods, but their misdeeds (actions motivated by greed, hatred, delusion, pride, and so forth) propel them to the sufferings of the lower realms of the hells, hungry ghosts (beings who live thousands of years tormented by hunger and thirst, unable to find anything to eat or drink), and animals. In most realms of samsara, beings have little or no opportunity to practice a spiritual path that could lead to liberation, or even buddhahood, for their existence is either too pleasant and distracting or too full of suffering. Only humans have the leisure to practice the dharma, but not all humans have the resources to do so—not everyone has access to the teachings of the Buddha or a situation that allows spiritual practice. Thus the leisures and resources referred to in verse 4 mean the opportunity to practice dharma, which is too valuable to waste.[3]

Merely having a precious human body is not enough, as we cannot practice dharma without faith and the wish to practice virtuous acts, called "Thoughts of the merits of the world" in verse 5. This comes from two factors: the buddhas compassionately teaching the dharma (called "the buddhas' power" in the verse) and sentient beings' merit, or habituation to virtue. For these two to come together is as rare and fleeting as a flash of lightning that briefly illuminates the night sky. For Shantideva, a deep appreciation of this precious opportunity is critical, as without it we will lack sufficient motivation to be diligent in our practice. From the perspective of Buddhist practice, these two stanzas are thus among the most important in the entire work.

THE SEEN AND UNSEEN BENEFITS OF BODHICHITTA

Shantideva now turns to the main topic of the chapter—a description of the benefits of bodhichitta. He does not explicitly define bodhichitta in this work—perhaps he felt his audience of scholars and practitioners at Nalanda already knew what it is. Generally, when we talk about bodhichitta, there are two types: ultimate and relative. Ultimate bodhichitta refers to the profound, direct realization of the empty nature of all phenomena. But usually the word *bodhichitta* refers to relative bodhichitta, the wish to become a buddha oneself in order to become able to bring all beings to buddhahood. This wish is rooted in compassion, which is traditionally characterized as the wish that others be free of suffering. All beings have the potential to feel compassion, but their compassion is usually limited to a small circle and rarely goes beyond a wish to alleviate visible suffering. The compassion of a bodhisattva is vast by comparison. It is the wish to free all sentient beings without any bias from all suffering and from its causes, not only in the present but until all beings have become buddhas. Merely wishing is not enough; their compassion impels bodhisattvas to actually strive to bring this about. This requires that they become buddhas themselves, which is no small task. Bodhichitta thus requires fierce determination and a tremendous amount of courage, so Shantideva devotes the rest of this chapter to describing the benefits of relative bodhichitta in order to inspire beginner bodhisattvas.

Shantideva presents two categories of benefits—the unseen benefits that will not become manifest until a future lifetime and the visible benefits that can be seen in this lifetime. Shantideva describes two unseen benefits. First is that bodhichitta is such a great positive force that it overwhelms the habituation to negative acts that would lead to rebirth in lower realms (verse 6). Likewise, bodhichitta will bring the bodhisattva the ability to bring infinite sentient beings to the lasting happiness of buddhahood, as the buddhas (called "the lords of sages" in the verse) have taught (verse 7). The visible benefit for this lifetime is that by rousing bodhichitta, one becomes a bodhisattva (verse 9). Often we use the word *bodhisattva* to refer to great beings such as Manjushri or Avalokiteshvara who have profound realization of the nature of reality, yet even ordinary beings who have the intention of bodhichitta but have not yet developed such realization are beginner bodhisattvas, children of the buddhas.

Shantideva next describes the specific benefits of bodhichitta using analogies. Traditionally, this passage is called "the six analogies," but properly speaking, there are five analogies and a reference to a sutra that lists many more. The first analogy compares bodhichitta to an alchemical substance that transforms ordinary iron into pure gold (verse 10). Similarly, bodhichitta transforms an impure body born out of karma and afflictions into the body of a buddha, a priceless jewel that is otherwise difficult to find.

The second analogy refers to a common trope of Buddhist literature: captains who lead companies of merchants through a perilous ocean journey to treasure islands where they can gather jewels to bring home (verse 11). Through their experience, the captains know how to avoid perils on the journey and are able to distinguish the gems of real value from worthless minerals, thus earning the trust of their companies. The captain represents the Buddha, who has the ability to discern the jewel of bodhichitta that has the true value of bringing the happiness that beings need and want. Just as merchants trust their captain, so too bodhisattvas should trust the Buddha and grasp hold of the precious jewel, bodhichitta.

The next three analogies relate to two essential aspects of Mahayana Buddhist practice: gathering merit and purifying obscurations. Gathering merit means instilling positive habits by thinking and acting virtuously—that is, in ways that bring benefit to ourselves and others. Bodhichitta is the most powerful method for gathering merit because it produces continuous results, unlike ordinary merits that produce a single result, like a banana tree that bears fruit only once (verse 12). Purifying obscurations means erasing the imprints our harmful actions and negative thought patterns have left within our mind stream. Shantideva specifically describes overcoming past misdeeds, both those strong negative actions that are certain to bring bad results and those that are indefinite— weaker negative acts that will produce results only when certain conditions come together. He compares the way bodhichitta purifies strong misdeeds and protects us from otherwise certain suffering to the way a hero protects travelers from bandits (verse 13) and likens the way it destroys the karmic residue of weaker acts to the inferno that destroys a universe at the end of an aeon (verse 14ab).[4] The last two lines of verse 14 refer to a long list of over two hundred analogies that the bodhisattva Maitreya taught to a student named Sudhana in the *Gandavyuha Sutra*.

Aspirational and Engaged Bodhichitta

When bodhisattvas rouse bodhichitta, they first develop the resolve, and once that is strong enough, they engage in action. Thus there are two types of relative bodhichitta, aspirational and engaged bodhichitta. Aspirational bodhichitta is the wish to achieve buddhahood for the sake of sentient beings, whereas engaged bodhichitta is actually engaging in the practices that will fulfill that aspiration (verse 15). Shantideva compares the difference between them to the distinction between wanting to go somewhere and actually setting out and going (verses 16). Just as the wish to go somewhere must precede actually going, so the wish of aspirational bodhichitta must precede engaged bodhichitta. Still, the benefits of aspirational bodhichitta are not as great as those of engaged bodhichitta (verses 17–19). Shantideva notes that the Buddha taught this in the *Sutra Requested by Subahu* in order to inspire people who are naturally more interested in the Foundation vehicle, which emphasizes achieving nirvana for oneself, to rouse bodhichitta and embark on the Mahayana path (verse 20).

Shantideva next describes the particular benefits of aspirational bodhichitta (verses 21–26), referring to the story of Maitra's Daughter, a previous incarnation of the Buddha. A merchant captain named Maitra and his wife Vasundara had several sons who all died in early childhood. In hopes of tricking the Lord of Death, they named their next son "Daughter." He survived and became known as Maitra's Daughter. While he was little, his father went to sea and died in a shipwreck, and Vasundara raised the boy on her own. When he came of age, Maitra's Daughter was determined to follow in his father's footsteps and go on a voyage to the treasure islands. His mother tried to prevent him, but he kicked her in the head and went to sea anyway. His ship was wrecked, and he washed ashore on an island. He eventually came to an iron city and met a man who had a terrible iron device attached to his head, boring into his skull and causing him tremendous pain. When he asked the man what happened, the man replied that this was the karmic ripening of kicking his mother in the head. At that moment, a voice came from the sky saying, "May he who is bound be freed! May he who is free be bound!" The device came off the other man's head and attached itself to Maitra's Daughter's head. As it drilled into his brain and he experienced unbearable agony, Maitra's Daughter also felt tremendous compassion for anyone who would ever have to endure this same torture. He made the aspiration that no one else would ever again experience such suffering of "sharp pains in sentient beings' heads" (verse 21). By the power of that aspiration, the device was released from his head and he was reborn in the realm of the gods.[5] Maitra's Daughter made an aspiration to relieve a single type of suffering, but bodhichitta has a vaster scope—it is the wish to free all infinite beings from their countless sufferings (verse 22). Furthermore, the wish of aspirational bodhichitta is rare—no one besides a buddha or a bodhisattva has it (verse 23), not even one's parents, gods of the sun or moon, Hindu rishis (sages), or creator gods such as the Brahmas, said to appear, one in each universe, according to some Hindu traditions.

Shantideva next extols the benefits of engaged bodhichitta, whose benefits far outstrip those of aspirational bodhichitta (verse 27). Among the many ways it helps beings (verses 28–30), the primary one is to remove the delusion that causes suffering and prevents beings from finding happiness. Engaged bodhichitta is also great because it does not depend upon reciprocation (verse 31) and because it has a vast scope in comparison to ordinary virtuous acts (verses 32–33).

Both aspirational and engaged bodhichitta are so powerful that they magnify the effects of actions that others do to bodhisattvas, whether negative (verse 34) or positive (verse 35). Even if someone tries to harm them (described as a "grave event" in verse 35), bodhisattvas feel such great compassion for that being that it is like adding fuel to the fire of bodhichitta, and their courage in their ability to purify that being's negativity blazes even brighter. Though a being who injures a bodhisattva may well experience a bad karmic result, the act makes a connection that will allow the bodhisattva to guide them to enlightenment in the future (verse 36).

Many of the benefits of bodhichitta that Shantideva describes are predicated on karmic cause and effect and past and future lives, and they have inspired generations of practitioners who believe in karma and rebirth. But people with a secular education sometimes find these ideas difficult. The traditional teachings on karmic cause and effect tell us to remember that our intentions and actions have

162 — A CONTEMPORARY GUIDE

effects beyond what we can see in the limited scope of our perception. Whether those effects extend beyond this lifetime depends upon whether our consciousness ceases at the moment of death or continues in some other form. That in turn depends upon the relationship between the mind and the body—what many contemporary thinkers call the "hard problem of consciousness." This is not an issue that science has yet been able to settle definitively, and there is much debate. If we keep an open mind and remember how limited our understanding actually is, we can appreciate the intelligence and compassion that underlie traditional teachings such as Shantideva's.

2. Confession: Preparing for the Bodhisattva Vow

***

B EING INSPIRED BY the benefits of bodhichitta is just the beginning. For Shantideva, we must become buddhas ourselves, and the first step toward that is taking the bodhisattva vow. The bodhisattva vow is such a powerful virtue that one must already be a good person to even consider taking it. Thus we must gather merit—deepen our habituation to virtue—to have the capacity to take and keep the bodhisattva vow. In Mahayana Buddhism, the most effective way to accumulate merit is considered to be the seven-branch prayer, a series of seven practices, each a greater source of merit than the previous. Thus Shantideva devotes this chapter and the first part of the third one to the seven-branch prayer as the preparation for taking the bodhisattva vow.

In the *Way of the Bodhisattva*, the seven branches are making offerings, going for refuge, confessing misdeeds, rejoicing in others' merit, requesting the buddhas to turn the wheel of dharma, supplicating them not to pass into nirvana, and making dedications.[1] The first three are described in this chapter; the remaining four are each taught briefly at the beginning of the next chapter. Shantideva writes in the first person, making the offerings and so forth himself. But he is also teaching by example, showing future generations how to rouse bodhichitta and take the bodhisattva vow.

OFFERINGS

The first of the seven branches is making offerings to the three jewels—the buddhas, dharma, and sangha of bodhisattvas. It is taught as a method to overcome any lack of faith or disrespect for the three jewels that would prevent us from taking the bodhisattva vow and also as an antidote for stinginess. It begins with actual offerings, described as "fine offerings" (verse 1), which means arranging the grandest offerings possible on a shrine. As Shantideva was a simple monk with little more than robes and an alms bowl, he also imagines taking everything in the world that has no owner and offering it to the buddhas and bodhisattvas (verses 2–7). He offers his body in this and all future lifetimes to be the "dedicated servant" of the buddhas and bodhisattvas, helping them bring happiness to sentient beings, as that is what pleases them most (verses 8–9).

Up to this point, Shantideva has offered material things and physical service. He then makes mentally emanated offerings, imagining that he is bathing the buddhas and bodhisattvas (verses 10–11) and offering them robes, scents, flowers (including the mandarava, which grows in the realms of the gods), incense, food, lamps, and many other beautiful and attractive things (verses 12–21). The bodhisattvas mentioned in verse 13—the Buddha's foremost heir Samantabhadra, the bodhisattva of compassion Lokeshvara (also known as Avalokiteshvara), and the bodhisattva of prajna Manjushri—are three of the "eight close sons," great bodhisattva disciples of the Buddha. His offerings to stupas and likenesses, or images (verse 21), are offerings to representations of the buddhas' mind and of the bodies of buddhas and bodhisattvas, respectively.

In verse 22, Shantideva imagines making what are called "unexcelled offerings." Bodhisattvas on the tenth level, such as Manjughosha (another name for Manjushri), are said in the sutras to be able to emanate great offerings through the power of their meditation. Though ordinary beings are not able to do this themselves, imagining it is said to be a source of great merit.

The next verses are offerings of praise (verse 23) and prostration (verse 24–25). When reciting these verses, it is traditional to visualize oneself surrounded by as many bodies as there are atoms in the universe, all prostrating in unison, to make the prostration more psychologically powerful. Physically and mentally paying respect to those who are worthy counteracts the obscurations of disrespect and a lack of faith and is also said to reduce pride.

GOING FOR REFUGE

The second branch, going for refuge (verse 26), is a foundational practice for all Buddhists as well as a necessary preliminary for taking the bodhisattva vow. *Going for refuge*[2] means recognizing that our ordinary ways of acting are unable to protect us from samsaric suffering. In fact, they perpetuate it. Buddhists see that the Buddha has taught methods that give beings refuge from suffering, so they go for refuge to him as their teacher. But buddhas have no superpowers to protect beings; it is by teaching that they offer refuge, so Buddhists go for refuge to their teachings—the dharma—as the path. It is also helpful to have guides to show the way, so they go for refuge to the sangha—beings who have practiced the path and realized the true nature of phenomena— as their companions on the path. The protection that the three jewels offer actually comes from us following the teachings and practicing the path.

Ordinarily one goes for refuge for the duration of this life only. In contrast, Shantideva goes for refuge until he reaches enlightenment's essence—that time in the future when he achieves buddhahood, no matter how many lifetimes away. His motivation is not only to find protection for himself but also to become able to give refuge to all infinite sentient beings. Likewise, we can think of the buddha, dharma, and sangha as individuals or teachings outside of ourselves—called "causal refuge"—or we can think of them as the type of being we will become or the qualities we will develop, which is called "resultant refuge." This means having the resolve to become a buddha and realize the dharma in full, and until we do so, to become a great bodhisattva ourselves. In essence, this is little more than a different name for bodhichitta.

CONFESSION WITH THE FOUR POWERS

Over the course of infinite lifetimes, sentient beings have invariably performed innumerable actions, some good, but many negative. This is bad enough in and of itself, but because of karmic cause and effect, misdeeds will ripen as suffering in the future, such as rebirth in the lower realms or sickness and deprivation if born as a human. As this would make it impossible to practice the path, bodhisattvas must purify themselves of that bad karma, and the method for doing so is confession with the four powers: the powers of remorse, support, making effort at the antidote, and resolving not to commit the acts again.

The power of remorse means to feel intense regret for the misdeeds and unvirtuous actions one has done. The passage on this power begins with a supplication to the buddhas and bodhisattvas (verse 27), followed by Shantideva's examination of his various misdeeds (verses 28–31). In addition to confessing those misdeeds he committed himself, Shantideva also confesses those he instigated others to do and those he rejoiced at others doing, since instigating and rejoicing in others' actions are taught to have the same karmic consequences as committing the acts oneself. Though Shantideva castigates himself severely for these acts, he also recognizes that they happened because of ignorance and his desires and aversions. Here, ignorance, confusion, and delusion all refer primarily to ego-clinging—grasping at our bodies and various thoughts, impressions, and emotions as if they were a unified, autonomous, permanent self. This fundamental confusion causes us to feel the root afflictions of desire for things that are pleasing, aversion for things that are displeasing, and ignorance for neutral objects. This then leads us to feel the various secondary afflictions of anger, pride, envy, doubt, and so forth, which prompt us to act in ways that harm ourselves and others or prevent us from practicing virtue.

For Shantideva, the ripening of karma was an unfailing fact that he had contemplated thoroughly and believed wholeheartedly. The intensity of his confessions comes from a deep dread of the suffering that he is certain his misdeeds will cause. In Buddhism, the ripening of karma is described as the natural result of a particular type of cause, not retribution or reward meted out by a judgmental deity. Just as cherry seeds bear sweet fruit and chili seeds hot, unpleasant or painful results of karma are a natural outgrowth of their causes—harmful actions motivated by defiled states of mind. But sentient beings do not have control over their minds and are unable to prevent themselves from acting unvirtuously. Suffering because of past actions is therefore not a sign of moral turpitude, nor is it a reason to feel guilt. Though Shantideva calls himself wicked, his deep regret is different from a discouraged sense of guilt, for he has full confidence that these stains can be purified, as evidenced by his exclamation "Wretched afflictions, cast out by the eye of prajna!" in the fourth chapter (verse 46).

In verses 32 and 33, Shantideva expresses his fear that he will die before he can purify his wrongs. Here and in many other passages throughout this work, death is personified as Yama, the Lord of Death, who represents the natural workings of karmic cause and effect and the impermanence of life. Shantideva then describes over the course of the next five stanzas (verses 34–38) how his offenses are pointless because of the ephemeral nature of samsara. The passage on the power of remorse concludes with Shantideva instilling in himself deeper regret by contemplating the terror and helplessness he will feel when his actions ripen upon him (verses 39–46).

The second power is the power of support, which means going for refuge to the three jewels and not forsaking bodhichitta (verses 47–53). Shantideva goes for refuge to the buddhas, the dharma, and the sangha of bodhisattvas, several of whom he calls by name, out of the sudden fear that arises from contemplating his misdeeds, and thus this passage has a different focus than the previous branch of going for refuge, which served as more of a general support for the practice of the path.

The third power is the power of applying the antidote—striving especially hard at virtue to counteract the wrongs one has done (verses 54–59). This involves recognizing the harm that misdeeds cause (even bringing ruin to all people who live in Jambudvipa, the continent where the Buddha appeared and taught the dharma, according to Buddhist cosmology) and doing what the Buddha taught, just as we would follow a doctor's advice. In particular, we should be careful to avoid misdeeds in the future, or else we will fall into the abyss of the lower realms.

The fourth power is the power of resolve, taught in the last six stanzas of the chapter (verses 60–65). First, Shantideva contemplates the reasons for regretting his misdeeds, and then he admits and confesses them all, both the naturally unwholesome (acts such as killing, which are misdeeds by their nature) and the disobedient (acts such as monks or nuns digging in the ground, which violate their vows but are not necessarily wrong otherwise). The actual power of resolve is expressed in the last two lines, where he resolves never to do such acts again. This final power is taught to be critical. Without it, confession will be halfhearted and hypocritical; it will lack the strength necessary to overcome habituation since beginningless time.

Throughout the confessions, Shantideva's language and imagery is strong—perhaps uncomfortably strong for some. To him, it is necessary to recognize the harmful nature of our wrongs and the terrible results they will lead to. Only when we view misdeeds with as much disgust and horror as we would view poison or metastatic cancer will we have enough impetus to actually confess them from our hearts, and only if we do that can they be purified. The idea that our wrongs can be purified and our faults corrected is central to Mahayana Buddhism. Buddhist literature has many stories of people who did terrible things and yet still achieved enlightenment in that lifetime, such as Angulimala, who murdered 999 people, and Milarepa, who killed thirty-five. The reason they could is that they recognized how horrible their actions were, sincerely regretted them, and confessed their misdeeds with the fierce resolve never to do any such act again. Softer language would not instill that sense of urgency. Furthermore, acknowledging how bad our own misdeeds are also helps us to develop empathy and compassion for others who have done similar acts. If we are to improve ourselves, we must honestly recognize our mistakes and make the resolve to change.

3. Embracing Bodhichitta: Taking the Bodhisattva Vow

WHILE THE OTHER chapters of the *Way of the Bodhisattva* each have their own, distinct topics, the third chapter reads more as a continuation of the previous chapter. It opens with the remaining four branches of the seven-branch prayer, presents the actual bodhisattva vow, and concludes with rejoicing in taking the vow as a method to stabilize and strengthen bodhichitta. In this way, the second and third chapters taken together present the entire ritual for taking the bodhisattva vow.[1]

Rejoicing

Often we feel envious of others who experience good fortune or do something good. We might feel resentment or think that they do not deserve it. Such thoughts arise out of habit, but they are antithetical to bodhichitta. Thus to take the bodhisattva vow, we must counteract them with their opposite, rejoicing.

Rejoicing means delighting in the virtuous acts others do and in the good fortune they experience as a result. It can be physical shivers and goose bumps, verbal expressions of appreciation, or mental feelings of sincere joy. Though simple, it is powerful—the Buddha said that it can bring even greater merit than actually committing the action. In the text, Shantideva first rejoices in the virtuous acts that ordinary, suffering beings do and in the samsaric happiness that results (verse 1). He then rejoices in virtuous acts that lead to liberation (verse 2) and in their results: enlightenment of the arhats (beings who have achieved the peace of nirvana for their own benefit), buddhahood, and the levels of the bodhisattvas—the ten stages of realization that bodhisattvas progress through from the time they first realize the nature of phenomena until they reach buddhahood (verse 3). Since the arhats have practiced the Foundation vehicle and the buddhas and bodhisattvas practice the Mahayana, Shantideva is rejoicing in the practice and fruition of all Buddhist practitioners, no matter what school they belong to. Finally, he rejoices in bodhichitta itself (verse 4).

THE REQUEST AND SUPPLICATION

The next two branches, requesting the buddhas to turn the wheel of dharma and supplicating them to remain without passing to nirvana, both involve making prayers to all the buddhas in all the worlds of any universe. According to the Mahayana, buddhas have clairvoyant powers and there is no near or far for them. It is said that buddhas can see all sentient beings as clearly as if they were in the palm of their hand and can hear their prayers, no matter where they are.

Until they achieve buddhahood, bodhisattvas still need to receive dharma teachings. But the buddhas do not automatically teach the dharma. They wait for someone to make a request first, in order to emphasize how rare the dharma is. When the Buddha Shakyamuni awoke to enlightenment, for example, he spent seven weeks without teaching, and only turned the wheel of dharma (that is, taught) when the gods Brahma and Indra came to earth and made the request. When Shantideva asks the buddhas to light the lamp of dharma (verse 5), it is in part so that he may receive teachings, but it is also for the benefit of all the beings in the realms where buddhas have awakened but have not yet begun to teach.

Next, Shantideva asks the buddhas not to pass into nirvana (verse 6). Through their realization, buddhas are said to be able to live indefinitely, but unless they are asked to remain, they will pass into parinirvana to teach their disciples impermanence. Near the end of the Buddha Shakyamuni's life, his attendant, Ananda, had three opportunities to ask him not to pass away but failed to do so each time. When the Buddha took ill and was nearing death, he told Ananda that had Ananda requested it, he would have stayed in the world, but since Ananda did not, he would pass into parinirvana, leaving this world. When a buddha passes into nirvana, it is as if "the eye of the world has been closed,"² and wandering beings (another term for sentient beings, who wander from realm to realm in samsara) are left in the blindness of ignorance.

Dedications

The last of the seven branches, making dedications, involves dedicating the merit of the previous six branches to bringing both temporary relief and ultimate freedom to all sentient beings. Shantideva begins by dedicating the virtue to eliminating the sufferings that all beings experience, listing in particular the sufferings of illness, hunger, and poverty (verses 7–10). In particular, he aspires to be able to nourish sentient beings in intermediate aeons of famine (verse 9), the ages just before a universe comes to an end when war, pandemics, and famine are inescapable and beings find it impossible to find any refuge. He also gives his body, belongings, and all his virtue to all sentient beings for them to use as they wish, as long as they do nothing that would cause them harm (verses 11–15). The reason is that he will have to leave them behind at the time of death, and if at that time he had not given them away, they would have done no one any good. By giving them away now, he is able to use them to bring great benefit to sentient beings. Shantideva revisits this idea of giving away everything to other sentient beings several times over the course of the work. It might perhaps seem a bit extreme; we usually think of keeping something just in case. But the sutras stress that bodhisattvas must not consider anything their own, including their own body, but instead dedicate everything to others' happiness.

After giving away his body, Shantideva makes aspirations to be of benefit to any sentient being who makes contact with him, whether in a good way or a bad way (verses 16–17). He prays to become whatever any sentient being might need, sustaining and supporting them in all ways (verses 18–22). In verse 20, he expresses an aspiration to become one of the magical items of Indian lore that fulfill all wishes. The wish-fulfilling jewel is the precious gem of a universal emperor that grants any wish made to it. A fine vase is charmed with mantras so that it will give forth whatever is needed. Great medicine contains all the vitality of the gods and demigods, so it can grant lifetimes, aeons in length. The heaven tree in the Heaven of the Thirty-Three gives the gods whatever they want, and the bountiful cow grants everything needed or wanted. These all produce whatever is desired without any thought, just as buddhas benefit beings effortlessly and free of any dualistic, conceptual thought. In this way, Shantideva is praying to be able to perform the vast activity of a buddha.

THE BODHISATTVA VOW

The seven branches are followed by the actual bodhisattva vow (verses 23–24). The form of this vow is a commitment to emulate the buddhas (again called "sugatas") and bodhisattvas of the past by arousing aspirational bodhichitta and then practicing the trainings step-by-step, which is engaged bodhichitta. The reason for this is that the only difference between sentient beings and buddhas is that at some point in the past, the buddhas aroused bodhichitta and then engaged in the training. There is no fundamental difference between the nature of a sentient being and a buddha, so any being can become a buddha by following their example. That process begins with taking the vow, so Shantideva here pledges to emulate the buddhas of the past. Nowadays, many Tibetan Buddhists also emulate him, reciting these two stanzas daily to rouse bodhichitta or using them as the text for the formal bodhisattva vow.[3]

Taking Delight

Once bodhisattvas have taken the bodhisattva vow, they need to strengthen and stabilize their resolve, and the method to do so is to take delight in their commitment (verse 25). Bodhisattvas rejoice for themselves because rousing bodhichitta brings them great benefit (verses 26–28), and they rejoice for others because it brings the ability to help others by eliminating suffering (verses 29–31ab), dispelling the afflictions and ignorance (verse 31cd–32ab), and giving bodhisattvas the capacity to bring benefit and happiness to others (verse 32cd–33).

The final stanza of this chapter is an exhortation to others to rejoice as well, because now that Shantideva has roused bodhichitta and taken the vow, he will eventually bring all sentient beings—gods, demigods, and all others—to comfort and joy in the short term and ultimately to buddhahood. Bodhichitta is the cause of buddhahood, so by rousing it now, it is certain that he will achieve that highest result. As the ancient Indian proverb says, "When the rain falls, the rice grows."

4. CAREFULNESS: THE BASIS OF PRACTICE

HAVING DESCRIBED HOW to take the bodhisattva vow, Shantideva spends the remainder of the *Way of the Bodhisattva* explaining how to keep it. In general, the bodhisattva's main practice is the six transcendences: transcendent generosity, discipline, patience, diligence, dhyana (a type of deep meditative absorption), and prajna. The Sanskrit word for "transcendence" is *paramita*, which literally means "gone to the other side." The transcendences go beyond, or transcend, both samsara and nirvana by being free of any concepts. For example, transcendent generosity means that when bodhisattvas give, they realize that the recipient, the giver, and the act of giving are all like dreams and illusions that appear through interdependent causes and conditions but have no true essence.

Before discussing the individual transcendences, Shantideva first explains the basis for the practice of all of them, carefulness— being conscientious about honoring the promise one has made in taking the bodhisattva vow and about keeping the precepts (verse 1). This requires valuing the vow and the precepts, reminding oneself of the consequences of letting it slip, and girding oneself with the confidence to follow through on it. All three of these require inspiration, so Shantideva spends much of this chapter contemplating the importance of keeping the vow.

BEING CAREFUL TO KEEP THE PROMISE OF BODHICHITTA

The path of the bodhisattva is daunting, and there is a danger that a bodhisattva might lose heart and give up, thinking that the goal of buddhahood is too lofty and difficult. For an ordinary commitment undertaken rashly, giving up or procrastinating might be reasonable (verse 2), but the bodhisattva vow is different. The buddhas and bodhisattvas have examined it with their prajna—their ability to distinguish what is from what is not—and found that it is not only possible but greatly beneficial (verse 3). Furthermore, Shantideva has himself taken the vow with due consideration. Were he not to fulfill his promise of inviting all sentient beings to buddhahood as his guests in the last verse of the previous chapter, he would have deceived all sentient beings (verse 4). As taught in the *Sutra Requested by Sagaramati,*

> For example, if a king or the king's ministers invite all the people of the town, telling them they will be given food, but neglect it and do not prepare any food or drink, they will have misled all those people. As the people received nothing to eat or drink, they would complain and leave. Likewise, Sagaramati, if a bodhisattva does not study and strive at the factors of enlightenment in order to liberate those who have not been liberated, free those who have not been freed, give respite to those with no respite, and bring those who have not reached nirvana to nirvana, that bodhisattva has not acted as promised and has deceived the world and the gods.[1]

One consequence of such deception would be to fall into the lower realms (verse 5–6). The sutras teach, for example, that someone who decides to give something away but does not out of stinginess risks the karmic result of rebirth in the realm of the hungry ghosts, who live thousands of years tormented by hunger and thirst, unable to find anything to eat or drink.

For Shantideva, the lower realms of the hungry ghosts, hells, and animals are neither more nor less real than the human realm. We humans grasp at the appearances of this world and our conceptions about them as solid and true, when in actuality the blinders of our ignorance, desires, and habitual thought patterns prevent us from seeing the transient, interdependent nature of existence. Because our ideas and reality do not mesh, we experience the gamut of suffering from barely noticeable stress to out-and-out misery, and we react in ways that perpetuate that suffering. Those beings who are born as animals, hell beings, or hungry ghosts likewise solidify their experiences as real and are unable see the true nature of existence. But due to their karma, the appearances they experience—a world filled with predators, a desolate landscape with nothing to eat or drink, or vast tracts of fire or ice filled with enemies—are more threatening and terrifying than the appearances humans usually experience, and their sufferings are greater. Even though the appearances of the lower realms are ultimately illusory, their inhabitants see them as real and experience tremendous suffering as a result. The dread Shantideva feels for such suffering is a powerful motivating factor that he refers to throughout this work.

Though it is usually taught that a bodhisattva who forsakes bodhichitta will fall into the lower realms for many aeons with little chance of liberation, there are exceptions (verse 7). One such was Shariputra, one of the great disciples of the Buddha who achieved the level of an arhat—someone who has eliminated all the afflictions and achieved nirvana. The Mahayana sutras teach that in a previous lifetime many aeons in the past, Shariputra also roused bodhichitta and vowed to achieve buddhahood. A mara (a type of demon that often tests the buddhas and bodhisattvas) asked Shariputra to give him his right hand. Shariputra gladly obliged, cutting off his own right hand, grasping it with his left, and offering it to the mara. But the left hand is considered unclean in Indian culture, so the demon took great offense and refused the gift. Discouraged by the difficulty of satisfying fickle beings, Shariputra gave up his vow. Yet many lifetimes later, he still became an arhat and one of the greatest of the Buddha's disciples. In this stanza, "the omniscient" refers to the buddhas, whose complete realization of emptiness means that they know the interdependence of all phenomena and of cause and result clearly.

In addition to leading to rebirth in the lower realms, breaking the bodhisattva vow diminishes the bodhisattva's ability to help others (verses 8–10) and delays their attainment of the bodhisattva levels (verse 11). For these reasons, in the first couplet of verse 12, Shantideva affirms his commitment to fulfill the promise of the bodhisattva vow.

BEING CAREFUL TO KEEP THE PRECEPTS

Just as bodhisattvas must be careful to maintain the basic motivation of bodhichitta, they also need to be careful to keep the precepts of the bodhisattva vow. There are many presentations of the precepts of aspirational and engaged bodhichitta, but in general, the precepts of aspirational bodhichitta can be summarized as never giving up on even a single sentient being. Bodhisattvas who think "I shall never help this being, even if I have a chance!" have violated their promise to bring all sentient beings to buddhahood and thus have broken the vow of aspirational bodhichitta. The precepts of engaged bodhichitta are to keep those of aspirational bodhichitta and to practice the six transcendences.

Shantideva does not specifically list the precepts in this text. Instead, he focuses on contemplations that create a strong and stable motivation, for it is easy to keep the precepts if the motivation is vivid. He contemplates how now that he has taken the bodhisattva vow, he will have little opportunity in the future if he does not practice bodhichitta now (verse 12). To remind himself to avoid committing misdeeds, he contemplates the sufferings of the lower realms, the inability to practice dharma there, and the preciousness of the fleeting opportunity given by a human body (verses 13–19). This culminates with a reference to the analogy of the blind turtle (verse 20) taught in the *Sutra of the Heap of Flowers*:

> Shariputra, for example, the entire earth becomes a single, great ocean, and in it there is a yoke with a single hole and also a blind turtle. The wind blows up and

down across that great ocean, and the blind turtle also surfaces briefly once every hundred years. It would be easier for that blind turtle who surfaces every hundred years to stick its neck through the single hole of that yoke than to be reborn as a human from a lower state. Thus it is extremely difficult to become a human from the lower states.[2]

Shantideva next reminds himself to be careful to practice virtue. He ponders how many misdeeds he has done in the past (verse 21), some of which, such as killing a parent, can be committed in the blink of an eye but lead to rebirth in the Incessant Hell, the lowest and hottest of the hells, where the inhabitants experience incessant heat and agony for unimaginably long lives. Misdeeds will not be exhausted on their own (verse 22), so Shantideva must put effort into cultivating virtue while he has the opportunity provided by his human life (verses 23–27b). Implicitly, he is teaching the two aspects of spiritual practice: giving up misdeeds, and practicing virtue.

In order to accomplish these two, bodhisattvas need to be careful to resist and then abandon the causes of bad actions, the afflictions—mental events that cause beings to commit negative acts and also taint any seemingly positive action they motivate. The word *afflictions*—a literal translation of the Sanskrit word *kleshas*—refers not only to manifest negative emotions and impulses such as anger, envy, scorn, and so forth but also to neutral states such as ignorance, doubt, or the view of a self—the construction of an idea of oneself as a real, independent person. It also includes mind states that do not rise to the level of an emotion but are inherently defiled. For example, butchers who slaughter animals all day long, inured by the frequent repetition of the act, may feel little or no emotion, but they are acting on an afflicted intent to kill. Thus the word *affliction* refers to a much broader scope of mental states than the phrase *negative emotion* does in everyday English. It means any mental event that disturbs the mind, preventing us from clearly seeing the true nature of reality. This is what Shantideva means when he asks rhetorically what he has inside of himself (verse 27).

Though not strong in and of themselves, the afflictions have gained control over us through habituation (verses 28–29) and cause us to commit acts that will lead to suffering far greater than an enemy could inflict (verses 30–31). Shantideva thus rouses the confidence that he will not slacken his efforts until the afflictions have been overcome and inspires himself to action with the imagery of heroic warriors entering battle (verses 32–44). After an ordinary battle, defeated enemies will bide their time in a neighboring land, waiting for an opportunity to seek revenge (verse 45). But the afflictions are not like that. Since they are mental, once they have been eliminated from the mind, there is nowhere for them to go to regain their strength. If we have not yet eliminated them, it is merely through our own lack of effort (verse 46).

When negative mind states are spoken of in the West, the focus is most often on how to prevent them from having an adverse impact on this life. There is rarely discussion of eliminating them completely. But the idea that the afflictions and other obscurations can be entirely eradicated from our mind stream is core to Buddhist thought and a major goal of practice. The reason they can be eliminated is that they are based on the delusion of ego-clinging and have no basis in reality. Though Shantideva uses battle imagery, the afflictions cannot be overcome by force or violence, nor is either necessary. Instead, afflictions are eliminated by turning the eye of prajna inward and seeing their true, empty nature.

In saying that afflictions do not dwell in objects (verse 47), Shantideva means that when we feel sexual desire for a beautiful person, for example, that lust does not exist in the other person's body, clothes, or manners. It cannot be found in our own eyes or other sensory faculties, nor can it be found anywhere between our senses and the person we feel it for. We might feel it as our breath catching or heart racing, but those are physical reactions, not the lust itself. No matter where we look, we cannot find anything we can identify as lust. It is the same with all the afflictions. Though they seem strong and real when we experience them, the afflictions are ephemeral and insubstantial, like an illusion. If we do not perpetuate them with our thoughts, they will subside on their own, and we will be unable to identify anywhere that they have gone. There is no reason to fear them. Instead, we must apply diligence to develop the prajna that allows us to see that they are empty of reality. Once we have truly seen that, they can never arise again to torment us in this life or the next. But we can see their nature only if we follow the Buddha's advice, so Shantideva closes the chapter by exhorting us to keep the precepts of the bodhisattva vow (verse 48).

These teachings on carefulness are central to the practice of a bodhisattva. Shantideva explicitly reminds the reader of them in the chapters on diligence and meditation, but carefulness is also essential for the other transcendences. It comes down to being careful of karmic cause and effect. For a bodhisattva who understands how actions lead to results, Shantideva's contemplations are similar to warnings to stay away from the edge of a cliff and not to touch live electrical wires—they help the bodhisattva make informed choices about how to act. Taking these teachings to heart gives them the self-control to act well, avoid suffering, and accomplish great ends.

5. AWARENESS: THE ESSENCE OF DISCIPLINE

IN THE NEXT several chapters, Shantideva explains the practice of each of the transcendences (except for generosity) in its own chapter, starting with transcendent discipline.[1] Discipline in Buddhism means keeping vows—the vows that primarily address conduct of body and speech such as the five lay precepts and monastic vows, or the vows that address motivation and ways of thinking, like the bodhisattva vow. But keeping vows requires guarding the mind, which motivates all our actions (verse 1).

The tools the bodhisattva uses to guard the mind are mindfulness and awareness. The word *mindfulness* is used broadly in English, but in traditional Buddhists texts, it refers to remembering what you should do and what you should not. In meditation, this would mean remembering the specific practice technique such as counting the breath, but in the context of this chapter, mindfulness is remembering what the bodhisattva vow allows and what it prohibits. Continually applying mindfulness brings awareness, which means simply knowing what is happening with your body, speech, and mind—being aware of whatever you are doing, saying, or thinking and not acting mechanically while your thoughts wander elsewhere. As the *Prajnaparamita in One Hundred Thousand Stanzas* says,

> When a bodhisattva mahasattva is going, they know, "I am going." When standing, they know, "I am standing." When sitting, they know, "I am sitting." When lying down, they know, "I am lying down." When they

have a pleasant or unpleasant physical feeling, they know it as it is.[2]

The fundamental reason for developing mindfulness and awareness is to be able to control the mind and consequently our physical and verbal actions. According to Buddhist teachings on karma, most misfortunes and dangers we encounter result from our past actions, and karmic actions are always preceded by an intention in the mind. For this reason, all wrongs depend upon the mind. An uncontrolled mind can incite evil actions that would cast us into the lowest hell, the Incessant (verse 2), while a mind held in check by the rope of mindfulness will restrain us from such actions and instead prompt us to act virtuously, protecting us from harm (verse 3). Even dangerous animals, enemies, demons such as dakinis (female demons who eat human flesh),[3] rakshasas (human-eating monsters who can be either male or female), and so forth arise from karma, our actions. Our karma originates in our volitions, which are mind, so controlling our mind will protect us from future danger (verses 4–5). Taming our mind will not necessarily save us if we are attacked by a tiger, lion, or elephant now (although there is a story of the Buddha taming a rampaging bull elephant in rut merely by his calming presence). Instead, it will prevent us from accumulating the karma that would lead to such dangers in the future.

Shantideva next teaches that everything—both positive and negative—depends upon the mind. In verses 6–8, he explains that the Buddha taught in the sutras that all sufferings arise from the mind, focusing on the sufferings of the hells. The appearances of the burning ground in hell or the lovers who seduce hell beings to cross through a forest only to be impaled on the long iron thorns of the *shalmali* trees were not made by a creator god. Instead, acting out of a wicked thought such as anger plants a poisonous seed in the mind that later, when conditions are right, rearises as the deluded perceptions of hell (verse 8).

Just as all faults depend upon the mind, so too do all qualities, including the six transcendences—generosity, (verses 9–10), discipline (verse 11), patience (verses 12–14), diligence (verse 15), dhyana or meditation (verse 16), and prajna (verse 17). What makes these six transcendent is not the external appearance or effect (eliminating poverty in the world or protecting all sentient beings from danger, for example) but the bodhisattva's intention (the willingness to give everything or the intention to refrain from doing harm). The "one clear thought" mentioned in verse 15 refers to a story from the *Mahaparinirvana Sutra* of a mother and daughter who were carried away by a flood. Each thought of the other with great love and prayed, "I hope she doesn't die!" but they both perished together. The result of their clear and loving thoughts was that both were born in Brahma's Realm, one of the abodes of the gods.

This portion of the chapter concludes with Shantideva reiterating that because the mind is the basis of everything good or ill, nothing is more important than gaining control over the mind (verses 18–21). Verse 21 is addressed specifically to his audience of celibate monks, but the advice applies to nuns and lay practitioners as well. Just as a monk who is mindful and aware will have no difficulty among people who might tempt him to commit an evil act or for whom he feels sexual attraction, guarding the mind with mindfulness and awareness is of utmost importance for anyone who keeps any vows, whether monastic, lay, or bodhisattva.

Developing Mindfulness and Awareness

Developing strong mindfulness and awareness requires that we first consider them to be important. Thus, Shantideva exhorts us to guard our mindfulness and awareness (verse 23) and gives five reasons why they are crucial: those who do not maintain mindfulness and awareness lack the strength of mind to act (verse 24), are unable to develop prajna (verse 25), are unable to practice pure discipline (verse 26), are in danger of destroying the virtues they have accumulated (verse 27), and will be unable to accumulate more in the future (verse 28).

He then discusses the specific causes for developing mindfulness and awareness, beginning with the five causes of mindfulness: keeping company with a teacher, receiving instruction from the abbot who gives the vows, fearing the consequences of lax mindfulness, having the fortune of a kind, good character, and respect and dedication for the path (verse 30). A further cause for mindfulness is the fear of embarrassing oneself before the buddhas and bodhisattvas (verses 31–32). Through meditation, the buddhas and bodhisattvas have cleared away their mental obscurations so that they are able to clearly see things that are hidden to ordinary beings. They are often described as having clairvoyant powers that enable them to know not only what any particular being has done in the past but also what is the best method to help that being. Recalling this helps practitioners to remember the buddhas frequently, which not only encourages them to avoid misdeeds out of fear of embarrassment but also inspires them to want to develop the same qualities themselves.

As mindfulness grows, awareness will also naturally increase (verse 33). Like a sentry who constantly checks to see if anything is amiss, mindfulness means remembering to constantly check ourselves to see whether the afflictions are trying to infiltrate our mind or not. That makes us aware—we know what is happening with our body, speech, and mind at that moment. This in turn strengthens our mindfulness of remembering what we should or should not be doing. In this way, mindfulness and awareness reinforce each other in a feedback loop.

At first glance, many of the reasons Shantideva gives for developing mindfulness and awareness, such as fear of future suffering and of embarrassment, seem negative. It might seem that the positive motivation of wanting to gain control over the mind or to help all sentient beings should be enough. In actual practice, though, this is often not the case. The afflictions are deeply ingrained, and we do not recognize them as harmful. This makes them hard to resist because people who see nothing wrong with anger, greed, and so forth are unlikely to take steps to combat them. Contemplating the negative consequences of the afflictions leads to the recognition of their poisonous nature in a way that focusing on positive reasons would not. Only then can we take steps to correct them and become better people.

TRAINING IN THE CONDUCT OF GUARDING THE MIND

As mentioned at the opening of this chapter, the practice of discipline is traditionally taught to entail keeping vows. In Mahayana Buddhism, there are primarily two levels of these vows: the vows of personal liberation, and the bodhisattva vow. The vows of personal liberation are vows of controlling one's body and speech to restrain from any harmful action. They include the monastic vows as well as the five lay precepts: giving up killing, stealing, sexual misconduct, lying, and alcohol and intoxicants. The bodhisattva vow is a vow primarily of the mind—of rousing the highest intention, achieving buddhahood to benefit all beings—but it is often taught that in order to take the bodhisattva vow, you must hold either a monastic vow or the lay precepts. This is because committing to avoid causing harm is a necessary first step before promising to benefit others. Thus bodhisattvas pursue three areas of discipline: the discipline of refraining from harmful actions, the discipline of gathering virtuous qualities, and the discipline of benefiting sentient beings.

The Discipline of Refraining from Harmful Actions

Though refraining from harmful actions primarily means keeping monastic and lay vows, Shantideva does not discuss their specific precepts. Instead, he emphasizes applying mindfulness and awareness and behaving in ways that are conducive to keeping control of our mind and intentions. He advises checking our intentions before acting and refraining from acting if they are tainted (verse 34), and he explains how we should perform ordinary activities such as walking in a manner that promotes mindfulness (verses 35–38). No matter what we are doing, whether a daily activity or sitting in meditation, we must constantly check our unruly mind to be sure it remains focused on thoughts of the dharma (verses 39–41).

Yet it is important not to be too tight with discipline; there are times of danger, celebration, or benefiting others when it is difficult to remain in the deep meditative concentration called samadhi (verse 42). In such situations, it is permissible to relax some minor disciplines, as taught in the *Sutra Requested by Akshayamati*, which says, "In times of generosity, withdraw from discipline and disregard it."[4] One should always observe the major precepts and never let go of mindfulness, awareness, and carefulness, but an act of generosity can be so beneficial that it outweighs discipline, just as a large heap of iron is more valuable than a small flake of gold.

In the next passage, Shantideva focuses on difficulties or actions that may seem minor but that decrease bodhisattvas' mindfulness and awareness, impairing their ability to keep the major precepts. He warns bodhisattvas not to be distracted from the tasks that they have set themselves to (verses 43–44), as that will decrease their awareness and lead to its opposite, the near affliction nonawareness. (Near afflictions are secondary afflictions that grow out of the root afflictions of greed, hatred, and delusion.) He advises them to avoid situations or actions that lead to distraction and carelessness (verse 45). He cautions fully ordained monks and nuns to be careful of the minor precepts (verse 46), including the rule against digging without a purpose. These precepts prohibit acts that although not negative in and of themselves, the Buddha forbade for monastics after specific events had occurred during his lifetime. Bodhisattvas must retain control of their mind in all situations, maintaining enough mindfulness, awareness, and self-control to be able to refrain from harmful or meaningless acts while remembering the Buddhist teaching of selflessness: What we think of as me is an idea we project based upon many different factors. We think we are a single being and in control, but in actuality there is no single "me" to be found anywhere in our body, mind, or elsewhere;

we are actually like an emanation or illusion that appears due to conditions (verses 47–57). Contemplating the precariousness and rarity of a human life where dharma practice is possible, Shantideva vows to keep his mind as stable as Mount Sumeru, the great mountain that Buddhist cosmology places in the center of the universe (verse 58).

The Discipline of Gathering Virtuous Qualities

Refraining from harm is not enough on its own; bodhisattvas also need to gather virtuous qualities—we need to develop our full potential for loving-kindness, compassion, and wisdom. But our attachments to our body and physical comforts often distract us from the practices that would develop those qualities. Such attachments are mistaken because the body lacks consciousness (verses 59–60), does little more than excrete filth (verse 61), has no essence that can be identified in any of its parts or anywhere else (verses 62–64),[5] and is of little use (verses 65–69b). Though this passage may seem on the surface like self-loathing, it is not, for Shantideva is quite clear that his body is not himself (as he will explain in chapter 9). Instead of pampering it, which would distract us from practice, he advises us to care for the body just enough to keep it functioning, but then put it to work to benefit beings (verses 66c–70).

Shantideva next discusses how bodhisattvas should conduct themselves with a tame and workable mind in order to mature their qualities. He advises being restrained and humble in everyday conduct (verses 71–73), being willing to accept advice (verses 74–75b), and praising others' good acts (verses 75c–78). He also describes how bodhisattvas should speak to or look at people (verses 79–80). He gives three factors in particular that increase the power of meritorious actions (verse 81): strong yearning; being motivated by the antidotes, bodhichitta and meditation on emptiness; and the field or recipient of the action. The field is so called because the recipient is like the field a meritorious seed is planted in—the more

192 — A CONTEMPORARY GUIDE

fertile the field, the greater a crop it will bear. An act of giving, for example, is far greater in merit if given to the field of qualities (the three jewels), the field of benefit (parents, abbots, teachers, and so forth), or the field of suffering (sentient beings who are stricken by poverty, illness, or misery). In this way, he advises bodhisattvas to put their efforts into activities that will bring the greatest benefit (verses 82–83).

The Discipline of Benefiting Beings

Once bodhisattvas have realized and thoroughly trained themselves in the previous two types of discipline, they should strive to benefit other sentient beings. But there are occasionally conflicts between the need to benefit a being and the precepts of their other vows. Verse 84 describes how, in such circumstances, the merciful Buddha allows bodhisattvas to break precepts that they otherwise should hold, as in the story of the bodhisattva Young Jyoti, who broke his vow of celibacy to marry a woman who threatened suicide otherwise. This does not, however, give bodhisattvas free rein to act any way they please. They should break precepts only if they have such great compassion and deep realization of emptiness that they are able to act without even the slightest taint of self-interest.

Shantideva teaches two ways that bodhisattvas benefit other beings: nurturing them with generosity, and protecting their minds. Nurturing other beings begins with generosity. Shantideva advises bodhisattvas to be moderate in their own needs and appetites and willing to give away everything except for the three dharma robes if they are monastic (verse 85).[6] Buddhist literature such as the Jataka tales (the stories of the Buddha Shakyamuni's previous lives) abounds with stories of bodhisattvas who are willing to give parts of their own bodies or even their lives, but Shantideva counsels beginner bodhisattvas not to harm or sacrifice their bodies when their realization is insufficient, as that would impede their development (verses 86–87).

Another way of nurturing beings is teaching the dharma (verses 88–90). Dharma should be taught only to people who are receptive to it. People who dress or comport themselves in disrespectful or arrogant ways (which in ancient India included wearing a turban, holding a status symbol such as a parasol, or swaggering about with a sword) may be unable to truly hear the teachings and should not be taught until their pride decreases (verse 88). Even when teaching, the bodhisattva must be careful to teach in ways that are equally respectful of all Buddhist schools and appropriate for the students (verses 89–90b). They must also avoid any appearance of impropriety. The instruction for a monk not to teach women unless a man is present is taken from a rule that the Buddha made one time after a bhikshu taught a woman alone in her home one day. Her husband came home and, enraged, erroneously accused them of illicit conduct. The Buddha then instructed his bhikshus not to teach women alone—that is, with no other man present—so that no one could unjustly accuse them, though he did grant that they could answer questions freely. In the present day, the analogue for this would be that dharma teachers should not only be scrupulous in taking and keeping lay or monastic precepts but also be respectful and sensitive to their students and careful to avoid even the appearance of impropriety or harassment, let alone any actual occurrence. Finally, dharma teachers must not disregard their own conduct by dressing sloppily or being uncouth and outlandish in their behavior or speech while teaching (verse 90c). They should also be careful not to use teachings about sutras or mantras to lead students astray out of selfish, prideful intentions (verse 90d).

The second way of benefiting beings—that is, protecting others' minds—means avoiding unclean, impolite, and offensive behavior that would cause people to lose faith or suspect them of inappropriate behavior. Verses 91 to 95 list many specific examples of this, some of which are still considered unclean or impolite in contemporary Western society, such as relieving yourself in drinking water (verse 91) or eating with your mouth open (verse 92) but some of which are not, such as pointing with your index finger, which was considered rude in Shantideva's time. (The tooth stick mentioned in verse 91 is a twig from a neem or other type of tree used as a natural toothbrush.) People might also lose faith if there is an appearance of improper relations, such as seeing a bodhisattva alone with someone else's partner. Though this comes from a rule for monks, the commentaries note that it applies to households as well. Above all, bodhisattvas must learn the local customs wherever they are and be certain to act accordingly because people who see one Buddhist behaving impolitely may well assume that all Buddhists are the same and lose faith in Buddhism. This passage closes with Shantideva advising bodhisattvas to strive to maintain awareness even as they fall asleep by lying on their right sides, in the same posture as the Buddha lay in when he passed into nirvana (verse 96).

Enhancing the Practice of Discipline

Though bodhisattvas should strive to have perfect discipline and to purify their mind (verse 97), that can be difficult before they achieve complete control over their mind. Occasionally, they will find that they have broken precepts, sometimes knowingly but often not. For this reason, Shantideva advises (verse 98) that bodhisattvas recite the *Sutra in Three Sections* six times daily to confess and purify their transgressions, using the four powers explained in chapter 2. He advises bodhisattvas to study extensively, both by reading and by being taught by a guru (verses 100–106). He illustrates this by referring to the story of Shri Sambhava told in the *Ornaments of the Buddhas Sutra* (verse 103). In this story, the youth Shri Sambhava and the young woman Shri Mati teach Sudhana that he should never be satisfied with a single virtuous act, aspiration, or attainment, no matter how great, because in order to achieve buddhahood, the offspring of the buddhas must practice limitless virtues for the sake of infinite beings.[7] Among the texts Shantideva recommends are two of his own works, the *Compendium of the Trainings*, a compilation of citations from the sutras on the same topics discussed in this work, and the *Compendium of the Sutras*.[8] In brief, he says that bodhisattvas should engage in all the practices that these sutras and treatises teach, acting properly in a way that will "guard the minds of worldly people"—first, by not offending them, and second, by inspiring them (verse 107).

Shantideva closes the chapter by briefly summarizing the characteristic of maintaining awareness—examining repeatedly what we are doing with mind and body—and by exhorting the reader to put these teachings into practice (verses 108–9). The habits of distraction are deep, and at first we must be vigilant to maintain awareness. But with enough practice, eventually awareness can become effortless.

6. Patience: Overcoming Anger

For bodhisattvas, whose practice centers on love and compassion, the most dangerous affliction is anger. Not only does it cause problems in this life but it also destroys the good that they have done in the past, negating the merit accumulated in millions of previous lives (verse 1). For Shantideva and others who believe in karmic cause and effect, this makes the practice of patience—bearing with others' insults and offenses without reacting in anger and forgiving those who have caused harm in the past—critical. But the urge of anger is hard to resist, and patience is far more difficult than any austerity such as refusing to wear clothes, living off cow manure, or harming one's own body to purify sin, as various non-Buddhist sects in ancient India did. At the same time, patience also brings far greater merit (verse 2). As it is said in the *Pratimoksha Sutra,*

> Patience is the greatest penance.
> Patience is sublime nirvana, taught the Buddha.[1]

Not only is anger a danger for future lives but it also robs us of peace of mind and happiness in this life and turns others against us (verses 3–5). Thus overcoming anger is of paramount importance if we want to find happiness (verse 6).

Anger cannot be merely repressed or blocked, for its poisonous seeds would remain in the mind stream, waiting to reemerge later. Instead, Shantideva teaches ways to retrain the mind and change the habits that lead to anger by examining and addressing its causes. Integrating new habits of understanding and compassion into our being can change patterns of anger into natural forbearance and forgiveness. But this requires perseverance and the mindfulness, awareness, and carefulness to actually apply these antidotes when anger first kindles in the mind, before it flares up and consumes us.

Retraining our mind begins with first identifying the cause that fuels anger and hatred, the displeasure that comes when our desires are frustrated or when undesired things occur (verses 7–8). To counter it, Shantideva counsels maintaining a cheerful attitude, for displeasure never serves any purpose (verses 9–10). But merely saying we should be cheerful does not prevent displeasure from occurring. Instead, it is necessary to examine its causes, which Shantideva describes as aversion to bad things happening to ourselves or our friends and family, and the opposite, aversion to good things happening to our enemies (verse 11). In other words, our worldly attachments and aversions lead to displeasure and anger, and the more we are able to diminish them, the less we will react in anger.

BEING PATIENT WITH PAIN AND HARM

Shantideva teaches three types of patience that we must practice when bad things occur to us. These include the patience of accepting suffering, the patience of contemplating the dharma, and the patience of disregarding harm. The patience of accepting suffering means being able to bear with hardship and pain. We must first acknowledge that pain is necessary for practice, as recognizing our own suffering leads to the wish for freedom from suffering and samsara (verse 12). Knowing our own suffering leads to the recognition that others also suffer in samsara and thus the wish to free them too. If we have such a noble goal, we should be able to be as forbearing as ancient Indian sects such as the Durga cults, who burned their own limbs or otherwise harmed themselves to achieve liberation, or the Karnatans from southern India, who were said to cut one anothers' heads off during lunar eclipses in a quest for renown and rebirth in heaven (verse 13). Learning to bear with discomfort now brings the ability to bear greater hardship in the future (verse 14). Just as worldly activities such as farming (verses 15–16) and war (verses 17–19) require bearing with suffering in hope of a future reward, so too does the bodhisattva's path. But worldly activities are essentially pointless—in battle, soldiers fight people who will eventually die anyway, so killing them is little different from killing a corpse (verse 20). In contrast, the path of the bodhisattva has a great purpose, the ultimate benefit for oneself and for others. Understanding this and the benefits of suffering (verse 21), bodhisattvas should rouse their courage to face pain and adversity.

The second type of patience is that of contemplating the dharma. Usually, we assume that people who harm or offend us are in control of themselves, and we think that they are injuring us intentionally. But sentient beings actually have little control over themselves, for they have no control over their own minds. Thus it is as illogical to get angry at sentient beings as it is to get angry at the causes of illness—the three humors of bile, phlegm, and wind according to ancient Indian medicine, or microbes, genes, and such in modern medicine (verse 22). When the conditions come together, sentient beings cannot help but feel and act upon anger, envy, greed, or contentiousness (verses 23–26). When we understand that they are not in control of themselves, we can feel more empathy for them, which makes it easier not to retaliate. In practice, this requires effort, but repeatedly contemplating this over time will gradually diminish and eventually overcome habits of anger. In effect, Shantideva is using the Buddhist teaching that there is no independent, autonomous self as a tool for practicing patience.

Many religions and philosophies say that humans have an independent, permanent soul, and we might think that therefore there is someone to get angry at. One such school is the ancient Indian Samkhya school, which explains that the appearances of the world are the manifestations of a primal substance appearing to a permanent, conscious self. Shantideva denies that either the self or the primal substance could arise intentionally and that a conscious self could be permanent or independent of the surrounding conditions (verses 27–28), and therefore neither deserves anger. Another school, the Nyaya, opines that there is a permanent self that is material, to which Shantideva retorts that such an inert self could never be involved in any action (verses 29–30), so there is no point in anger at it either. In brief, all sentient beings and all external things are subject to conditions, and no one is truly in control of themselves. Their appearance as individuals who act willingly is an illusion. When we realize this from our hearts, we will no longer get angry at illusory people and things (verse 31).

But if we say that people and anger are unreal and illusory, then we might think who—what illusory person—could avert what unreal anger (verse 32)? If it is all an illusion, practicing patience by averting anger would seem illogical. Shantideva responds that because anger and suffering arise in dependence upon conditions, they can be stopped: preventing their causes will stop them from occurring. Even though suffering is illusory, those who experience it think that it is real, and therefore it is logical to try to stop it.

Verses 33 and 34 summarize this passage on the patience of contemplating the dharma and segue to the patience of disregarding harm. Shantideva introduces it by discussing how those who harm us in fact deserve our compassion (verses 35–38) and how anger at them makes no sense, for they have no control over themselves (verses 39–40). Shantideva illustrates this with the vivid analogy of getting angry not at the stick used to beat us but at the person who wields it (verse 41). Likewise, we should get angry not at the person, who like the stick has no control over themselves, but at the delusion, hatred, and anger that compel the person.

Shantideva also contemplates that he himself has a share of blame for the harm he receives. Not only does it occur because of similar harms he inflicted on others in the past (verse 42), he also experiences it as suffering due to his own clinging to his body (verses 43–44). Since it is the ripening of his own misdeeds, getting angry at the other is senseless (verses 45–46). (The sword-leaf forests mentioned in verse 46 are a specific hell where one seeks refuge in a forest from the heat and packs of wild dogs only to be sliced by the sharp blades on the leaves of the trees.) Indeed, those who seem to harm us actually benefit us by giving us the opportunity to practice patience, whereas they will experience suffering such as the hells as the karmic result of their actions (verses 47–49). Though it might seem that we would be at fault for the aggressor falling into hell, if we practice patience, not only do we have no desire to send them to hell but we also have the virtuous quality of the intention to be patient, thus protecting ourselves and preventing further harm to our assailant (verse 50).

In addition to being patient with those who harm us physically, we also need to be patient with insults and criticisms (verses 52–53), other people expressing displeasure (verse 54), people preventing us from gaining material things (verses 55–61), and people criticizing us and causing others to lose faith in us as bodhisattvas (verses 62–63). Primarily, this passage advises us to look clearly and see that these indignities cause no real harm. The mind itself cannot be harmed by anything outside itself, life is transient and fleeting, material possessions must be left behind at death, and no matter how upsetting they are, words are no different from echoes, arising from conditions and perishing without a trace.

Practicing Patience for Those Who Harm Loved Ones

When people or things we love or revere are harmed, our habit is to react with anger, so Shantideva next describes how to practice the patience of contemplating the dharma and disregarding harm in such situations too. He teaches that when people destroy symbols of the buddha and dharma such as statues and texts (verse 64) or when people we respect or love are harmed (verse 65), the aggressors have no control over their minds and are driven by ignorance and the afflictions. He urges us to practice the patience of contemplating the dharma, using the same logic as taught above.

Shantideva then turns to the patience of disregarding harms inflicted on our loved ones, using similar logic as for disregarding harms to oneself. It is not logical to single out sentient beings for anger when nonsentient phenomena such as natural disasters and disease cause harms as well (verse 66). He notes that both the initial aggressor and the person who responds with anger act from ignorance (verse 67) and that harms befall our loved ones because of their own karma. Therefore the proper response is loving-kindness, not anger (verses 68–69). We should be like the bodhisattva Maitreya who, in a previous lifetime when he was named Dridhamati, radiated such great loving-kindness that his merely stepping across the threshold of a house would cause all the beings who lived there to develop the samadhi of loving-kindness. Shantideva also counsels remembering the negative results of anger (verses 70–71), the positive results of patience (verse 72–73), and the great purpose that patience will serve (verses 74–75). His analogy of a prisoner being relieved to have a hand cut off instead of a head (verse 72) might seem barbaric nowadays, but execution and amputation were common punishments in ancient India for crimes that might merit little more than a fine, community service, or short imprisonment in many countries today.

Rejoicing in Adversaries' Good Fortune

A third area where anger and resentment easily arise is when we see our enemies experience success and good fortune. We might feel a knot of envy or anger when an adversary is recognized and praised, for example. But as Shantideva points out, praising others brings happiness to oneself (verses 76–77), while refusing to rejoice out of envy and anger will lead only to our own suffering (verses 78–79). Shantideva compares this to stopping paying wages to employees, who will then stop working or otherwise retaliate. Refusing to rejoice similarly prevents the bodhisattva from receiving the rewards of merit and good fortune in this lifetime (the seen) and in future lifetimes (the unseen). Shantideva also points out that refusing to rejoice when an enemy finds happiness (verse 80), honor (verse 81), or material gain (verses 82–83) contradicts the bodhisattva vow. Not only that, there is no effect on the bodhisattva whether an adversary receives a gift or not (verses 84–86), and thus no reason to feel envy. "To vie against those who have performed merit" (verse 86) means that since people receive gifts as the ripening of earlier meritorious actions, someone whose mind is filled with envy is trying to compete with someone enjoying the ripening of their merit. But this is futile: it's like a moth competing with a lamp flame; it will do nothing more than exhaust their own merit.

BEING PATIENT WHEN DESIRES ARE FRUSTRATED

Another common cause of anger is our desires being frustrated. When our desires are clearly negative, such as when we want an enemy to be ruined or disgraced, Shantideva notes that they will lead to us being cooked in cauldrons in hell without having any effect on the enemy (verses 87–89). Other times, our frustrated desire is for our own worldly gain and respect, but attachment to praise and fame is pointless and childish (verses 90–97). Being thwarted in our pursuit of praise and fame can actually be beneficial because it protects us from the lower realms and helps us achieve liberation (verses 98–101). It is also possible to get upset at people whom we think disrupt our spiritual practice, such as people who disturb us when we meditate, but the real obstacle is getting angry ourselves (verses 102–3). We can no more develop patience without offensive people than we can grow corn without seeds. Difficult people are a cause of our patience (verse 104), and they actually provide us with an opportunity, just as a beggar provides the opportunity to be generous and an abbot or abbess gives an opportunity to take monastic vows, traditionally called "going forth from home to homelessness" (verse 105).

Bodhisattvas hold all sentient beings dear because only if there are other beings can they develop the qualities of loving-kindness, generosity, discipline, and so forth. In particular, the enemies and people who frustrate bodhisattvas provide them the greatest benefit (verses 106–8), as there is no opportunity to practice patience without them (verses 109–11). Both sentient beings and buddhas are like fields from which virtuous qualities grow (verse 112): generosity, discipline, and patience grow from the field of sentient beings, and faith, pure intention, and the powers and so forth grow from the field of buddhas. As the Buddha said in the *Sutra of Pure Aspiration*,

> Because of the fields of sentient beings
> And fields of buddhas, I attained
> The excellent harvest of the crop
> Of a buddha's infinite qualities.[2]

In this respect, sentient beings are as worthy of respect as the buddhas, even if not their equal in terms of the qualities of wisdom and compassion (verses 112–18). Sentient beings give us an opportunity to practice kindness, and that is their greatness (verse 115). Offerings to "those with loving-kindness"—parents, dharma teachers, abbots, and so forth who have treated us with love—are said to bring especially great benefit, but even giving a mouthful of food to an animal is a powerful source of merit. All sentient beings have the same fundamental nature as the buddhas or guardians, and they all have the capacity to achieve buddhahood. Respecting them is thus the best way to fulfill the wishes of the stalwart friends, the buddhas and bodhisattvas, and to repay their kindness (verses 119–26).

THE RESULTS OF PRACTICING PATIENCE

Shantideva concludes the chapter on patience by describing its benefits: pleasing the buddhas (called "tathagatas" in the verse), fulfilling one's own aim of achieving buddhahood, and relieving suffering (verse 127). He compares practicing patience and respecting sentient beings to the way in which wise people do not retaliate against repressive and cruel agents of a king because that would incur the full force of the king's wrath and lead to even more suffering. Likewise, reacting in anger against sentient beings will incur the full force of karmic consequences, personified as the keepers of hell, and displease the compassionate buddhas (verses 128–30). The last few verses describe the ultimate and temporary results of practicing patience: reaching the state of buddhahood (verse 132), enjoying recognition and happiness in this lifetime (verse 133), and gaining beauty, health, prestige, and the riches of a chakravarti, a universal emperor who rules over entire continents without ever harming another sentient being (verse 134).

For many readers, anger is the emotion that presents the greatest difficulties in their lives. The contemplations and methods that Shantideva describes are effective remedies for anger, but they take time and effort to work. They require constant mindfulness and awareness so that when situations arise where you might get angry, you have enough presence of mind to try to put them into effect. It is a slow process, and you may feel that there are more defeats than victories at first. But with enough effort, anyone can apply these techniques and train themselves to be more patient and forgiving.

7. Diligence: Enthusiasm for Practice

DEVELOPING PATIENCE BRINGS a capacity to forbear difficulty and hardship that increases bodhisattvas' ability to strive at their practice, but that alone is not sufficient. Enlightenment and the other qualities of a buddha or bodhisattva can come only from hard work and effort—no supreme being or buddha can bestow them on anyone. Diligence is like the wind, which makes all things move, according to ancient Indian physics: without diligence at their practice, bodhisattvas cannot gather merit and make progress down the path (verse 1). Ordinarily, the word *diligence* refers to any sort of industriousness, including that found in business, sports, and such. But worldly work is usually done out of self-interest and concern for this life and is thus, for a bodhisattva, considered a type of laziness. Here, then, *diligence* means zest or enthusiasm for virtuous practices such as generosity and for study, contemplation, and meditation (verse 2a). Thus Shantideva devotes this chapter to inspiring us to such enthusiasm, discussing first how to overcome its primary impediment, laziness.

OVERCOMING LAZINESS

Since diligence is enthusiasm for virtue, anything contrary to that is considered laziness—a broader definition than is used in everyday English. Shantideva identifies three types of laziness (verse 2b–d). The first, clinging to bad actions, includes neutral pastimes such as amusing oneself with games in addition to obviously harmful actions. The second, sloth or indolence, which promotes carelessness, is what we normally think of as laziness. The third is self-disparagement, the self-defeating attitude of thinking that you lack the ability to achieve enlightenment. These three originate not only from what we would usually imagine, such as enjoying sleeping and lolling about, but also from not taking the suffering of samsara to heart and not developing a genuine wish for liberation (verse 3).

This is particularly true of the first two types of laziness, clinging to bad actions and sloth. As antidotes for them, Shantideva prescribes contemplating impermanence (verses 4–10), the sufferings of samsara and karmic cause and effect (verses 11–13), and the precious opportunity we have as humans (verse 14). But contemplation alone is not sufficient; we also must gather the accumulations (verse 7) of merit and wisdom—train ourselves in virtuous thought and action and as a result develop greater understanding and wisdom—and we must do this now, while we have the chance. Otherwise, we will end up like the gods who fritter away their entire lives, only to suffer excruciating regret and psychological pain when they realize that they are about to die and foresee their next rebirth (verse 13). Addressing the laziness of clinging to bad actions in particular, he also admonishes bodhisattvas to remember that what we do to amuse ourselves brings temporary pleasure at best but distracts us from what will bring true and lasting happiness, the practice of true dharma (verse 15).

The third type of laziness, self-disparagement, stems from thinking that we are unable to achieve buddhahood and balking at the difficulties of the path. Countering this involves practicing the bodhichitta meditations taught in the next chapter (the equality of self and other and exchanging oneself for others) and rousing diligence with the techniques taught later in this chapter: the four forces, purpose or perseverance, and self-control (verse 16). But it also requires understanding that buddhahood is possible. As the Buddha (called the "Tathagata" in the verse) taught in the *Sutra Requested by Subahu*, all sentient beings, even the lowliest insect or worm, can achieve buddhahood if they put in the effort (verses 17–18). The Jataka tales include stories of the Buddha's previous lifetimes as animals, and the vinaya scriptures relate stories of animals who feel faith, die, and are reborn as humans who then achieve nirvana. Humans already have an intelligence that animals do not, and there is no reason why they cannot achieve enlightenment if they try (verse 19).

Practitioners might also be daunted by the difficulty of the bodhisattva path, especially when they hear the many stories of bodhisattvas giving away parts of their bodies or sacrificing their lives for others' sake. Shantideva reassures them that the pain of such acts of generosity is minor compared to the suffering of samsara (verses 20–24) and that anything becomes easy with habituation (verses 25–26). The methods the Buddha taught are gentle: training the mind, starting with small gifts and the cultivation of love and compassion. Eventually bodhisattvas see that their body is no different than any other material object in that it is not itself sentient and does not truly belong to anyone; they occupy it like a guest staying a night or two in a hotel room. No longer attached to their body as "mine," they are able to give it freely. For bodhisattvas, such acts are actually the greatest pleasure (verses 27–28). The power of their bodhichitta is so strong that they surpass not only ordinary people but also the shravakas, the disciples of the Buddha who follow the path of the Foundation vehicle (verse 29). The inspiration of bodhichitta will carry the practitioner past the doubt, disappointment, fear, and self-centered focus on their woes and inadequacies to the joys that unbounded altruism brings here and in the next life (verse 30).

THE FOUR FORCES

Next is the main practice of diligence, which Shantideva summarizes as the four forces. Ancient Indian armies had four divisions— chariots, elephants, cavalry, and infantry—and monarchs would use all four to defeat their enemies. Likewise, bodhisattvas triumph over adversity and achieve buddhahood with the four forces of long-ing, steadfastness, joy, and deferring (verses 31–32). Contemplating the suffering of samsara and the benefits of diligence brings longing, which in turn leads to steadfastness, the pride of confidence in one's ability to overcome the afflictions. As that increases, the bodhi-sattva's joy in diligence also grows, but occasionally the bodhisattva must rest and defer an activity or leave it behind when completed.

The description of the first of the forces, longing, begins with Shantideva examining himself and seeing how little progress he has made in abandoning the faults (verses 33–34), accomplishing the qualities of a buddha (verses 35–36), and engaging in activities that benefit others (verses 37–38). His point is not to discourage himself. Instead, he notes that his lack of progress and the suffer-ings he has created are due to his insufficient longing or desire to practice the dharma (verse 39). Since longing is produced by under-standing karmic cause and effect (verse 40), he contemplates how virtue leads to happiness and misdeeds to suffering (verses 41–43) and then contrasts the results of virtue (rebirth in a pure realm where bodhisattvas who have purified their karma are born with all the favorable conditions for dharma practice in the presence of buddhas who continually teach the Mahayana) with the results of nonvirtue in two parallel, lyrical stanzas (verses 44–45). Shan-tideva closes this passage by exhorting the bodhisattva to long for virtue (verse 46ab).

The passage on the second of the four forces, steadfastness or pride, begins in verse 46 with a reference to the *Dedications of Vajradhvaja*, a chapter of the *Ornaments of the Buddhas Sutra*. In this sutra, the bodhisattva Vajradhvaja describes the indomitable resolve of a bodhisattva mahasattva (great being), saying,

> When the sun shines, it is not turned back by the fault of blindness. It is not turned back by the faults of dust and smoke in the sky or of separate shadows or uneven mountains. Likewise, the bodhisattva mahasattva's pro-found and vast mind and indomitable thoughts are not

turned back by the faults of sentient beings' suspicious ways. They are not turned back by the fault of unruliness. The armor of enlightenment is not stopped by the depravity of sentient beings.[1]

There are two aspects to such steadfastness. The first is being steadfast at the outset—making certain before beginning a task that you can carry it through and committing fully to it if you decide to begin (verses 47–48). The second aspect is being steadfast while acting, which involves meditating on three types of pride (verse 49): the pride of action, the pride of the afflictions, and the pride of ability. Throughout this passage, Shantideva plays on two senses of the word *pride*. Sometimes it refers to the afflicted pride of thinking oneself different from, or superior to, others, and sometimes it means the antidote pride, the confidence of the bodhisattva—the courage of knowing that you have the capacity to perform bodhisattva activity yourself without being overwhelmed by the afflictions. Such courage is crucial for diligence, but bodhisattvas must continually check that it is not corrupted by afflicted pride, which must be abandoned.

In the following stanzas, Shantideva then describes each type of pride, though in a different order than he presented them in verse 49. First, the pride of action is the confidence that you can accomplish something yourself without relying on others (verses 49c–51). Second, the pride of ability is confidence in your capacity to overcome obstacles and achieve buddhahood (verses 52–59). Shantideva illustrates it with the example of a crow strutting like a garuda (a powerful mythical bird that eats poisonous snakes and naga spirits) around a dead snake, which it would never do were the snake alive. Likewise, the downfalls (violations of the precepts) will act as if they were strong when mindfulness, awareness, and carefulness lapse, but if bodhisattvas have pride or confidence in their ability to maintain these three, the downfalls will have no chance. Third, the pride of the afflictions (verses 60–63) is the confidence that you are able to overcome the afflictions by thinking,

"The afflictions will not get the best of me! I will destroy all the afflictions!"

The third of the forces is the force of joy, the bodhisattvas' insatiable pleasure in their actions (verses 64–67). Though Shantideva compares bodhisattva activity to games and play, there is a great difference, as ordinary pleasures are ethically neutral and often encourage negative actions. Like honey on a razor, they are sweet at first but lead to suffering. The activity of a bodhisattva, by contrast, is so inherently satisfying and brings such good results that bodhisattvas feel a natural enthusiasm for immersing themselves in it.

The last of the four forces, the force of deferring (verse 68), means knowing when to step back. There are two situations when this is necessary. The first is when you get fatigued. The commentaries explain that bodhisattvas exhausted by work, study, and contemplation should rest in samadhi meditation, or if they have not yet achieved stable meditation, they should recite inspirational prayers or read sutras. It is taught elsewhere that even sleeping can be virtuous if you first set the firm intention that you are resting in order to be able to continue bodhisattva activity. The second situation is when you have completed a task. At such a time, you should let go and move on to whatever awaits you next. No matter how satisfying an activity, pushing too hard or clinging to it too strongly once it is done can become an impediment. Sometimes putting it aside is best.

INCREASING DILIGENCE

The chapter closes with a passage describing two qualities that help increase diligence: perseverance and self-control. Shantideva illustrates perseverance with a series of vivid examples—the fray of battle (verses 69–70), the spread of poison (verse 71), and a snake slithering into your lap (verse 73)—that demonstrate maintaining mindfulness and awareness with single-minded focus so as to never be distracted by the afflictions. But there are times when this can be difficult. Shantideva counsels that in such situations, bodhisattvas should seek out a meeting with a learned, ethical, and experienced spiritual teacher to learn what would be appropriate (verse 75).

Verse 72 illustrates the degree of focus necessary with the story of King Prayota of Avanti, who arranged a performance of song and dance as an offering for the arhat Katyayana. Katyayana sat through the performance with his faculties gathered inward in deep meditation, not sensing what was happening around him. When the king asked whether the singing and dancing were good, Katyayana replied that he had neither seen nor heard them. The king said, "It is possible that someone whose faculties are gathered inward might not see, but how could you not hear them?" Katyayana replied, "King, is there anyone in the dungeon who is condemned to death?" The king replied that there was. Katyayana then said, "Then give that man a bowl filled to the brim with mustard oil and position behind him an executioner with his sword drawn. Tell him that if even a single drop of oil spills, his head will be cut off that very instant, but if none at all spills, he may go free. Then have him circle the city, led by singers and dancers." The king did as Katyayana instructed, and the prisoner circled the city without letting a single drop spill. Katyayana then asked the prisoner, "Was the singing and dancing good?" The prisoner replied, "I didn't hear or see anything at all. I was terrified for my life— forget about watching or listening!" The prisoner was freed, and Katyayana said to the king, "Great King, if this person could thus focus his faculties inward for fear of just this one life, why would it not be possible for us to gather them inward to overcome suffering until the end of samsara?"

The second quality that increases diligence is self-control (verses 76–77). Bodhisattvas should be steadfast at the outset, considering their actions carefully before beginning, and remember the teachings in the chapter on carefulness in order to have the strength to complete their actions. Doing so makes their body and mind light, workable, and easy to direct. Just as a breath of wind directs which way a tuft of cotton blows, the wind of enthusiasm gives bodhisattvas the self-control that allows them to accomplish all virtuous activities. A mind tamed in this way is the most excellent result of diligence.

8. Meditation: Cultivating Bodhichitta

A s bodhisattvas tame their minds through the practice of diligence, they become progressively better able to focus their minds on virtue and practice meditation. At this point, they need to learn to rest in samadhi (deep meditative concentration) because if their minds wander in distraction, they will fall prey to the afflictions (verse 1). Thus Shantideva devotes this eighth chapter to meditation.

There are many different styles of meditation, each with its own purpose, but generally there are two main types: shamatha, which develops the stability of the mind, and insight, which leads to clearly seeing the nature of reality. Though some commentaries on the *Way of the Bodhisattva* teach that this eighth chapter teaches shamatha and the next teaches insight, Shantideva does not discuss techniques of shamatha meditation (such as counting the breath) in this chapter. Instead, he primarily describes meditations on bodhichitta, which have aspects of both shamatha and insight in that they both bring stability of mind and lead to a deeper understanding of the true nature.

Before practicing meditation, we need to reduce the distractions that prevent us from resting in samadhi. Though strong meditators are able to meditate undistracted in any circumstances, beginners are easily distracted by external conditions and their own attachments. They lack the mental stability necessary for developing the capacity to benefit others and need to isolate themselves from distractions. Thus Shantideva advises seeking two types of solitude: solitude of body, which means forsaking society to go to an isolated retreat, and solitude of mind, which counters the habits of discursive thought by reducing desire and attachment (verse 2).

SOLITUDE OF BODY: LEAVING SOCIETY

Before bodhisattvas go off to an isolated retreat, they should first deeply consider the reasons for doing so, or their motivation will not be strong enough to sustain them. Consequently, they need to contemplate how attachment to partners, family, and friends and craving for material things, worldly achievements, and recognition prevent them from developing stability in meditation (verse 3). If bodhisattvas are to overcome the afflictions and develop the qualities that will allow them to benefit others, they must practice both shamatha and insight meditation in conjunction—that is, they must have the stability of mind to rest undistracted while looking directly at the ultimate nature. This requires that they first achieve stable shamatha meditation (verse 4). To develop this, they must apply the antidote to attachment by contemplating the problems it causes not just in this lifetime but in future lives as well.

Though we might wish we could be with our loved ones forever, our connections to them are transient and our attachment to them causes many problems. In addition to disturbing the mind and leading us to squander this precious opportunity (verses 5–8), such attachment weakens the bodhisattva's world weariness, the sadness that comes from realizing the suffering and futility of samsara. In addition to distracting bodhisattvas, attachments lead them to unvirtuous action and the lower realms (verses 9–14). Throughout this passage, Shantideva describes ordinary, worldly people in pointed terms. He calls them childish because they chase the impulses of their id like little children and labels them fools because they do not know what is best for themselves. His aim is not to insult them but to decrease the bodhisattvas' attachment. He advises bodhisattvas to be kind but detached when dealing with others (verses 15–16), alluding to a verse from the *Pratimoksha Sutra*:

> Just as a bee sips nectar from
> A flower without injuring
> Its scent or hue, then flits away,
> So does the Sage move through the town,
> Not thinking about others' faults
> Or what they've done or have not done.[1]

Just as attachment to loved ones is a hindrance, so is craving for material gain, recognition, and so forth. Shantideva describes how they lead to suffering in future lives while themselves being ephemeral and pointless (verses 17–21), and he reiterates the difficulty of getting along with sentient beings (verses 22–24). When bodhisattvas take all this to heart and withdraw from the world, they can develop the stability that will allow them to achieve the qualities needed to benefit sentient beings.

This passage is followed by a hymn to the joys of meditating in a solitary, isolated retreat, speaking in particular of the forest hermitages favored in ancient India (verses 25–37). He also describes one of the main meditations for reducing attachment, repulsiveness meditation. It was a common practice in ancient India to lay corpses in a charnel ground, and Buddhist monks and nuns would watch the corpses decompose, meditating on how their own bodies have the same nature as a corpse. This decreases the practitioner's attachment to their own body and lessens their desires, which then brings stability in meditation.

Shantideva also describes how spending the rest of his life in solitude will benefit him at the time of death. Not only will his death not disturb any loved ones by causing them grief, their mourning will not distract him from the recollection of the buddha, dharma, and sangha that should be foremost in the mind at the time of death (verse 36).

SOLITUDE OF MIND: GIVING UP
DISCURSIVE THOUGHTS

Even in physical solitude, discursive thoughts provoked by desires, especially sexual ones, can prevent the meditator's mind from settling into shamatha (verses 38–39). Once again, Shantideva teaches repulsiveness meditation as the antidote, but instead of contemplating the likeness of our own body to a corpse as he did previously, he instructs us to imagine our beloved's body as a corpse, nothing but a skeleton that has always been dependent upon conditions and never had any true control over itself (verses 40–42). Though the body may be alluring when clothed in fabric (such as the veils worn by women in some parts of India in Shantideva's time), we find it terrifying when it is exposed by scavengers picking at its flesh (verses 43–44). He asks why we find it attractive now when it is no different from food for scavengers (verses 43–46) or a zombie animated by a spell or spirit (verses 47–48). Not only is the beloved's body a source of filth (verses 49–64), clothing and perfuming it do not change its foul nature (verses 65–70), and chasing after it brings exhaustion in this lifetime and suffering in the next (verse 71). In the last couplet of verse 59, "the field" refers to the mother's womb, "the seeds" to the mother's blood and father's semen (the ancients had no way of seeing the actual ovum or sperm and thought that fetuses grew from a mixture of blood and semen), and "what grew them" to the placenta, all of which were considered unclean in ancient India.

Shantideva was a monk addressing an audience that consisted primarily of other monks and writes from the perspective of a heterosexual man. Even so, the meditation applies to anyone we find attractive—the dangers of lust and attachment are the same, regardless of gender or orientation. No matter how attractive they seem on the surface, all human bodies (including the meditator's body, as Shantideva points out in verses 56 and 61) are the same in being bags of skin filled with filth, cages of bones bound by sinews and plastered with the mud of flesh. But we do not see that. We view an attractive person's body as an object of sexual desire that will bring us pleasure, or we mistake it for being a person who can fulfill our needs. We might even do both. Either is a misapprehension of what that body truly is, and repulsiveness meditation acts as an antidote to the lust and attachment that underlie both.

It might seem that viewing another's body as repulsive would shame or otherwise cause harm to that person. But this meditation is the practitioner's own private contemplation; no one else need know that they are doing it. Like all Buddhist contemplations, it is focused inward toward decreasing and eliminating the meditator's own afflictions. By reducing lust and attachment, it counters the habit of viewing others as objects of sexual gratification and thus allows the meditator to treat all other people with respect, loving-kindness, and compassion. Instead of hurting others, it is a basis for actually gaining the ability to help them.

Shantideva then describes the cost of obtaining our desires, material as well as sexual, in this lifetime and the next (verses 72–84). The passage on withdrawing to solitude and cutting the ties of attachment closes with a lyrical depiction of the joys of meditating in retreat, where the natural features of the landscape are as luxurious as any palace and the comfort of being content with what you have surpasses the pleasures of the rich and powerful (verses 85–88).

MEDITATING ON THE EQUALITY OF ONESELF AND OTHERS

Shantideva now turns to the primary topic of this chapter, the meditation on bodhichitta. He presents two meditations: the meditation on the equality of oneself and others, which uproots the habit of cherishing oneself more than other sentient beings, and the meditation on exchanging oneself for others, which replaces the habit of self-cherishing with the habit of cherishing other sentient beings more than oneself. He teaches the meditation on equality of oneself and others first, beginning with a brief overview of the meditation: Since all sentient beings are the same in wanting to avoid pain and wanting to be happy, bodhisattvas should not consider their own needs primary but instead protect all sentient beings as they would protect themselves (verses 89–90).

You might wonder how a single individual could possibly bring happiness to infinite numbers of sentient beings; we might think that all we can do is make one person, ourselves, a bit happier. But that is actually a delusion. Any happiness we might find for ourselves is transient, and our attachment to it is a cause of future suffering. That one self we cling to is actually a conglomeration of many parts—limbs, organs, fluids, cells, and so forth—which we protect as if they were one, single thing. Similarly, we can protect sentient beings of all different kinds because they are all equal to us; their wish for happiness is no less important than our own (verse 91). Shantideva's logic hinges upon the idea that the only difference between our own happiness and suffering and others' is that we cling only to our own, not to others'. Even though our own suffering does not affect others, it is unbearable to us because of ego-clinging, and we are relieved when someone else alleviates it (verse 92). Likewise, though others' suffering does not affect us, it is also unbearable to them because of ego-clinging, and they are also relieved when it is alleviated (verse 93). There is no essential difference between our suffering and others' and thus no real reason to prioritize ourselves over them.

Shantideva next describes the basic meditation (verse 94) and the reasons for practicing it (verses 95–96). Following this, he presents others' objections to this meditation and his responses (verses 97–107). The logic of many of these verses is based upon the basic Buddhist idea of the lack of a self. Though we ordinarily think that we are single beings who are distinct from others and who have an enduring existence, Shantideva argues that this idea is a fiction. Our bodies and minds are aggregates of atoms and mental events in a constantly changing continuum that we mistake for a single me (verse 101). It is like a column of marching ants: we might say that they pass by in a series, but there is no series or column separate from the individual ants. Likewise, the continuum of our mind is a series of discrete moments that pass one after another, but there is no single thing to which they all belong. The situation is the same with our body, which is an aggregate of all the atoms that comprise it. That aggregate does not exist separately from those atoms, just as there is no battalion apart from its individual soldiers. Our idea of an enduring self that experiences suffering is ultimately a fiction, but ordinary beings do not realize that, which causes them suffering. That fiction must be dispelled, no matter whose it is, and suffering must be dispelled, no matter who experiences it.

In response to the objection that compassion is too painful, Shantideva alludes to the story of the dharma teacher Supushpachandra told in the *King of Samadhis Sutra* (verse 106).[2] The forest-dwelling Supushpachandra realized that he would benefit many beings if he went to teach dharma in the city but that doing so would endanger his life. He went to the city regardless and spent a week teaching the inhabitants. On the seventh day, the king and his family went for an outing. While the king relaxed in a park, his wives and children came across Supushpachandra and listened to him teach the dharma. When the king woke up, he found them listening with such great respect and devotion that he was enraged and had Supushpachandra executed right then and there. A week later, Supushpachandra's corpse had not decayed even the slightest, and the king, filled with regret, built a stupa in his honor. Many aeons later, that king awoke to enlightenment as the Buddha Shakyamuni.[3]

The passage concludes with four stanzas describing the benefits of meditating on the equality of oneself and others (verses 107–10).

MEDITATING ON EXCHANGING ONESELF FOR OTHERS

The meditation on the equality of oneself and others lays the groundwork for meditating on exchanging oneself for other sentient beings, which is the basis for the *tonglen* (giving and taking) meditation commonly practiced in the Tibetan tradition. In this meditation, we replace the ordinary ego-clinging of fixating on our body and mind as me or mine with the antidote ego-clinging of instead viewing all other sentient beings as me or mine. This leads us to cherish them more than we cherish ourselves.

Shantideva first observes that we think of our body as ourselves only due to habituation. According to the Buddhist scriptures, at the moment of conception, the consciousness of a recently deceased being enters the mixture of the mother's blood and father's semen in the uterus and clings to it, thinking, "That is me!" (verse 111). As the embryo grows into a fetus and is eventually born, the habit of clinging gets more entrenched, but it has no basis other than that initial fixation. With enough effort, habits can be changed, so Shantideva instructs us that instead of clinging to this body and mind as me, we should cling to all other sentient beings as me (verse 112). The point of this meditation is not to actually become another being, which is clearly impossible and would create even greater delusion than ordinary ego-clinging. Instead, the aim is to replace our egoistic attachment to this body and mind with cherishing others as more important than ourselves (verse 113).

Though Buddhism usually teaches that ego-clinging is to be eliminated, here Shantideva instructs us not to eliminate it but to replace our habitual object of ego-clinging (this body and mind) with another (all other sentient beings). As he will say in verse 136,

> I'll give myself away to others
> And cling to others as myself.

Though this is still ego-clinging, it is transformed by skillful means into an antidote that frees even beginners from deeply ingrained habits of grasping at a self, without requiring much logical analysis. As Dharmakirti of Suvarnadvipa taught,[4] meditation on selfless-ness or emptiness alone can be dry and ineffective, just as a flower cannot grow from a seed planted among stones. Flowers grow best in soil rich with dung, and bodhichitta grows best when fertilized with the manure of ego-clinging.

Following this brief overview, Shantideva then presents the logic for the practice (verses 114–20), the reasons for practicing it (verses 121–25), and a comparison of the benefits of practicing it with the dangers of not (verses 126–35). Verse 118 illustrates how no anxiety or discomfort is too insignificant for a bodhisattva's compassion by referring to a passage from the *Gandavyuha Sutra* in which the bodhisattva Avalokiteshvara blesses his name, saying,

> I bless it so that when any sentient being, even if insane,
> merely remembers my name, no suffering of any kind
> will occur for them, and they will not even feel fearful
> or scared of being in crowds.[5]

Shantideva begins his discussion of the actual technique of exchanging oneself for others with a four-verse overview of the technique (verses 136–39), followed by three separate meditations on envy, competitiveness, and pride. The meditation on envy involves exchanging yourself for those beings who are inferior to you in social or economic standing, education, abilities, and so forth, and thinking enviously of this body and mind (that is, the one you would ordinarily cling to as yourself). You imagine how you (as the inferior) would feel when this body and mind receive honors and gain and so forth (verses 141–46), which counteracts habits of seeing inferiors as lowly and contemptible. Then Shantideva explains exchanging yourself for your equals and meditating on competitiveness, imagining then how you (as the peer) would try to take everything good from this body and mind and leave them a laughingstock. This deflates ordinary, afflicted competitiveness (verses 147–50). Lastly, you exchange yourself for a superior and meditate on pride. As the superior, you look at this body and mind with contempt and sarcastically put them in their place to defeat the habits of envy (verses 151–54). The point of all three of these meditations is that instead of competing against or comparing ourselves to others, we need to vie against, counter, and overcome our own ego-clinging.

Following the description of the meditations, Shantideva returns in verse 155 to the ordinary understanding of self and other and counsels his mind to continue training in cherishing others more than himself. He first speaks in a gentle manner (verses 155–66), reminding himself to always benefit others and to take the lowest position. He advises his mind not to let ego-clinging become strong and impetuous but to be instead like a young bride sent in an arranged marriage to her husband's family, where, as the lowest in status, she would be shy and fearful of upsetting her in-laws (verse 166). Likewise, our mind should be shy of committing misdeeds, afraid of the lower realms, and restrained, our attention turned inward toward improving ourselves instead of minding others' business. Shantideva then takes a sterner tone, castigating his mind to make it submit to his wish to cherish others more than himself (verses 167–72). He concludes this passage by recalling that attachment to the body is the source of all faults (verses 173–84).

Dispelling the Obscurations to Meditation

No matter what type of meditation we practice, there are obscurations that prevent the mind from resting stably and clearly. Buddhist texts teach five obscurations, though Shantideva explicitly mentions only one, the obscuration of sleep and torpor, which prevents the mind from being clear (verse 185). The others are excitement and regret, which prevent the mind from resting tranquilly; malice, which prevents it from resting comfortably; pleasure seeking, which keeps it from becoming workable; and doubt, which prevents it from resting one-pointedly. Meditation manuals and the oral tradition of instructions provide techniques to remedy these five, but Shantideva does not. Instead, he provides general advice about being diligent and maintaining the carefulness taught in chapter 4 (verse 186) because unless meditators appreciate the importance of good meditation, they will be unlikely to apply specific techniques even if they know them.

In the last stanza (verse 187), Shantideva summarizes the entire chapter by resolving to turn away from the wrong paths of selfish pursuits, find solitude of body and mind, and rest his mind in meditative equipoise on the right focus, bodhichitta. As bodhisattvas apply themselves in this way, their practice gradually becomes deeper and they achieve stability—the aspect of shamatha meditation. This allows them to remain undistracted from the meditations on the equality of oneself and others and on exchanging oneself for others, which break down the ego-clinging of cherishing oneself over others. They are then able to see the fundamental equality of all beings and gain a better understanding of the true nature—the aspect of insight meditation. This union of shamatha and insight prepares the bodhisattva for the realization of emptiness, the topic of the next chapter.

9. PRAJNA: UNDERSTANDING THE TRUE NATURE

ALL OF THE practices taught in the previous chapters are directed toward realizing the true nature of phenomena. They tame the bodhisattva's mind and make it workable, giving it the clarity needed for such realization, but they are not sufficient on their own. Bodhisattvas also need to develop the prajna that directly sees that nature, the emptiness of all phenomena. However, without first developing limitless compassion and practicing generosity, discipline, and the other transcendences, any understanding of emptiness gained would only be dry and intellectual, not a true, transformative realization. Such a realization is necessary because only a direct realization of emptiness can entirely uproot the afflictions, which lead to suffering, and overcome the habits of dualistic thought, which prevent us from achieving buddhahood. Thus the bodhisattva must strive to develop the prajna that clearly sees the ultimate nature (verse 1).

The word *prajna* (not infrequently translated with the English word *wisdom*) is often used in colloquial and narrative contexts as a synonym for intelligence, but it has a specific meaning, the capacity to discern dharma from nondharma. On a basic level, it refers to discerning which thoughts and actions are beneficial and should be adopted and which are harmful or perpetuate suffering and thus should be abandoned. On a deeper level, it is understanding the interdependent causes and conditions that make our actions, words, and thoughts beneficial or harmful, and on the most profound level, it refers to discerning the empty, selfless nature. Prajna accompanies every cognition, though it can be quite weak or even mistaken, as when people do stupid or harmful things. Thus bodhisattvas need to strengthen their prajna by study and contemplation until it can become transcendent—until it is free of any conception of self or other and gives them the ability to directly perceive the ultimate nature.

This chapter outlines the basic arguments bodhisattvas must study to develop such prajna. At first, they must gain an understanding through listening—traditionally, they would receive detailed teachings from a teacher. Then they should analyze it thoroughly until they find certainty based on their own understanding—not merely by having blind faith in someone else's words. Finally, they must meditate on that basis until they see the nature themselves. In this way, there is a three-step process of developing prajna through listening, contemplating, and meditating. It takes a long time but leads to stable realization.

The nature of its topic makes this chapter more philosophical in tone than the other chapters. This is compounded by the fact that Shantideva taught it at one of the great ancient universities to an audience of monks and scholars who were already familiar with many of the ideas. Furthermore, Buddhist philosophical texts such as this chapter were not intended to provide detailed explanations. Instead, they give synopses of the main arguments in an easily memorizable form; teachers would explain the intricacies to their students orally. All of these factors make this chapter more challenging than the rest of the *Way of the Bodhisattva*.

The first step to finding a way into this chapter is to have a basic idea of the different schools Shantideva discusses in this chapter. From its very beginnings, Buddhism has coexisted with many different religions and philosophies, and over time, several schools developed within Buddhism as well. As mentioned in the introduction, the Buddhist schools largely fall into two categories, the Foundation vehicle and Mahayana. The Foundation vehicle spread widely first and eventually divided into eighteen different schools based on language, details of monastic practice, and tenets. These schools shared many commonalities, and

Shantideva does not discuss them individually, except for one, the Vatsiputriya, which had some unique tenets concerning the individual self.

The Mahayana began to develop in the second or first century BCE, and by Shantideva's time, two major Mahayana schools, the Mind Only and Middle Way, were well established. The Mind Only takes its name from its basic position: Everything we perceive or think of is a mental projection. It is only mind, but mind itself ultimately exists. The name Middle Way refers to taking the middle way between the extremes of existence and nonexistence: any idea of something truly existing or not truly existing is merely a conceptual fabrication, and in actuality, nothing can be proven to either exist or not exist. This view originated in the work of the great Buddhist master Nagarjuna (second century CE), and Shantideva is considered to be one of his philosophical heirs. Later Tibetan masters called both of them "Consequentialists" because their style of argument was to point out the logical inconsistencies and absurd consequences of their opponents' positions. This chapter is considered a major presentation of the Consequentialist view.

Shantideva also addresses four non-Buddhist schools: the Samkhya, Vaisheshika, Nyaya, and Mimamsa. (The Samkhya and Nyaya were both mentioned in chapter 6.) He does not treat any of them at length, only refuting a few of their positions as they relate to points in his own larger argument.

Historically, the Samkhya school was the earliest. It originated a few centuries before the Buddha's time with the teachings of the sage Kapila and eventually developed a complicated metaphysics that has had an enduring influence in Indian philosophy. Not only are there still adherents of the Samkhya, many elements of its thought were incorporated into the yogic philosophy of Patanjali and later schools including Kashmiri Shaivism.

The Vaisheshika school was likely the next in historical sequence. Its founder, the sage Kanada, cannot be precisely dated; he likely lived sometime between the sixth and second centuries BCE. This school developed an atomic theory of matter and classified all phenomena into six categories in a way that bears some similarity to Aristotelian philosophy. Strongly realist, it can be considered a reaction to the reductionist Buddhist approach exemplified by Shantideva's logic in this chapter.[1]

The Nyaya school grew out of the Vaisheshika and shares many of its positions. Traditionally, its founding is credited to Akshapada Gautama, who may have lived sometime between the sixth century BCE and the second century CE. The Nyaya is known for its rigorous system of logic and epistemology, which strongly influenced all subsequent Indian thinkers, including the Buddhist logicians Dignaga and Dharmakirti.

The Mimamsa was an orthodox Hindu school that was primarily concerned with the proper performance of ancient Vedic rituals. It originated in the works of Jaimini, most likely no earlier than the fourth century BCE.[2] Shantideva does not address it at length, specifically refuting only one of its positions.

The views of all these schools, Buddhist and non-Buddhist, are sophisticated and subtle; it would be difficult to give any of them justice in a short synopsis. Instead, the specific points that Shantideva raises will be discussed in basic terms as they come up in the chapter. The middle portions of the chapter, where most of the refutations of other schools are found, are not easy at first. Understanding them takes repeated study and contemplation. A broad idea can be gained with a bit of effort; a true comprehension of the subtleties can take a lifetime. But the opening and closing of the chapter present important ideas without the debate that complicates the rest of the chapter. The first seven stanzas describe, in addition to the two truths, how one develops a proper view in stages, each progressively more profound. The last seventeen stanzas (verses 151–67, discussed under the heading "The Results of Meditating on Emptiness" below) describe why contemplating emptiness is not merely an academic or intellectual exercise and how it is inextricably linked to compassion. A good understanding of these opening and closing passages helps the middle of the chapter come into clearer focus.

THE TWO TRUTHS

All schools of Buddhism distinguish between the superficial way things appear to ordinary beings and the actual nature of how they really are. The way things appear is called the "relative truth," and the actual nature is called the "ultimate truth" (verse 2ab). When we use the word *truth* in English, we might think that it means something akin to a law of physics or a cosmic principle, but in Buddhism, it does not. The very things we experience and our ordinary mind itself are relative truth—there is no relative truth separate from our experience. The true nature of those very same relative things is the ultimate truth. These two truths are not separate from each other or from anything we experience. The ultimate cannot be found anywhere other than in relative appearances, for it is their very nature, and the relative can never appear separate from its nature, no more than there can be fire separate from heat. As the Buddha said in the *Heart Sutra*, "Form is empty. Emptiness is form. Emptiness is not other than form; form is also not other than empty."

But ordinary beings do not see the ultimate truth because it cannot be seen by mind (verse 2cd).[3] What Shantideva means by *mind* is the ordinary sensory consciousnesses and thinking mind. (In this work, as in many Buddhist texts, *mind* is synonymous with *consciousness, cognition*, and *awareness*, when that latter is used as a translation of the Sanskrit word *samvedana*. When *awareness* is used in the sense described in chapter 5 of knowing what is happening in your body, speech, and mind, it is translating the Sanskrit *samprajana*.) These consciousnesses are accompanied by a dualistic sense that there is a knower who is observing an object that is other than itself. There is a subtle clinging to the object and the observer as being real—that is, as distinct, enduring, singular, and autonomous entities. This obscures the true nature, so ordinary beings can see only the relative truth.

For this reason, Shantideva distinguishes between two types of people: yogis, who see the deeper reality, and ordinary people, who cling to appearances as truly existing as they appear (verse 3ab). Ordinary beings project names and ideas onto images that, like a movie, flit through their minds so rapidly that they confuse the stream of images for something real and persistent, even though nothing real can be found on a fundamental level. This leads to attachment to pleasant appearances and aversion to unpleasant ones. This in turn prompts beings to act in ways that perpetuate the cycle of samsaric suffering. In contrast, yogis have a deeper understanding of the true nature. They realize that appearances are a constant flux of interdependent causes and conditions similar to dreams, illusions, or characters in a movie. They therefore can confute or disprove the misunderstandings of ordinary people (verse 3cd).

Beings have varying degrees of obscuration, and this creates distinctions in their intellect and understanding; it is difficult to leap directly from the confusion of an ordinary person to the realization of a noble bodhisattva or buddha. For this reason, the Buddha taught different stages, like a series of stepping-stones to bring practitioners from an ordinary, worldly understanding to the ultimate yogic view (verse 4). For example, the repulsiveness meditation taught in the previous chapter is a yogic view, but it is just a preliminary step toward the realization of impermanence, interdependence, emptiness, and so forth. The Buddha taught each step using analogies that worldly people can accept and understand, even though yogis do not necessarily view those analogies as ultimate truth. Therefore disagreements between yogis and ordinary people come down to the degree to which they cling to appearances as truly existing in the way that they seem (verse 5).

The two truths can be difficult to accept at first because the world seems so consistent and real to us. But it is not in actuality. We can see this easily from extreme examples: The ground seems firm and stable by its very nature until it bucks beneath your feet in a strong earthquake. If the firmness and stability of the ground were real and part of its inherent nature, the ground could never not be firm and stable. Or, after a traumatic event or sharp knock on the head, someone's personality can change so drastically that their loved ones wonder whether they are the same person any more. If their personality were an essential part of their nature, it could never change so abruptly. If we look more closely, we can see that the ground is constantly eroding and shifting and that people's personalities develop and change over their entire lifetimes. We merely do not notice because they happen so slowly, on such a subtle level. Over time, the changes are dramatic. When we look at the progression from fetus to baby to child to adult to senior citizen, each of those stages are so different that we cannot say it is all one and the same person. What we think of as fixed and real depends on interdependent causes and conditions in the same way that a movie or a dream does. As it changes gradually, we do not notice, and assume that it is the same thing. But just as a movie stops if there is a power outage or a dream upon waking, when conditions change, what seemed real—the stability of the ground or a personality—ceases. This is why Shantideva says relative things are not real. Still, they appear. The Middle Way is not nihilism. The point is not to deny our experience but to understand its nature more deeply so that we can cut through the cravings and aversions that come from our misapprehensions and attachments.

Foundation Vehicle Objections to the Two Truths

For Shantideva and the Middle Way school, such analysis can be carried down to the infinitesimal to show that nothing, not even atoms (or the subatomic particles of modern physics), has any true, independent existence. But other Buddhist schools dispute this on the grounds that if there were no real building blocks out of which our experience were made, then we could have no experience. For that reason, Shantideva here addresses their objections, beginning with those of the Foundation vehicle.

Foundation vehicle schools agree that the appearances of this life are relative truth and thus fictitious. But they state that these fictions have a real basis: Matter is comprised of atoms, and our minds of cognitions (basic awareness) and mental factors (the various qualities of cognition such as attention, feeling, and emotion). Atoms, cognitions, and mental factors are all impermanent, arising and perishing in each infinitesimal instant, but in that instant they do exist in ultimate truth, according to the Foundation vehicle. The atoms and cognitions in each instant act as causes for the next atoms and cognitions, which are similar enough that we mistake them for enduring over time. Atoms combine with their neighbors to form objects large enough to be perceived as shape, color, and so forth, and we mistake them for larger objects such as grains of sand, pebbles, rocks, or mountains. Without the real basis of atoms or momentary cognitions, we would experience nothing. There would be no sentient beings or buddhas even relatively. No one would gather merit by making offerings to the Buddha, and no one would be reborn to experience the results of karma. Thus momentary atoms and cognitions must exist because we do see things made of them, and, moreover, the Buddha taught them, they say.

From Shantideva's perspective, the Foundation view is a step on the path, but it cannot lead to buddhahood on its own because it still has a degree of conceptual clinging. He argues that perceiving something with the senses does not prove that it exists ultimately because sensory perception still relies on societal designations that what we see is a cup, a table, the color red, or so forth (verse 6). The Buddha did teach in the sutras that things such as atoms, consciousness, and so forth exist momentarily (verse 7) but that was for people who are not ready for the profound view. Ultimately, they cannot be established to arise and perish in each instant (for reasons Shantideva will explain below) and thus are not truly momentary. This Foundation view is a level of yogic relative truth that takes us a step closer to suchness, the nature of things, so the Buddha taught it in order to introduce the worldly to the profound gradually (verse 8).

Shantideva also disputes the claim that karmic cause and effect need a real basis. Even though causes and results are illusory, they occur consistently on a superficial level and sentient beings cling to them as real. Merit from offering an illusory buddha (called a "victor" in the verse) still creates causes and conditions and will lead to a positive, albeit illusory, result (verse 9). Likewise, sentient beings do not need a true basis in order to cycle through samsara. As long as there are the conditions that produce it, the illusion of a sentient being will continue (verse 10) and that being will be confused until they realize the illusory nature of their existence. Merely lasting for a long time does not make them less illusory, just as the characters in a long movie are no more real than the characters in a short one.

Being illusory does not mean that there are no virtuous acts or misdeeds. Killing an illusory being created by an illusionist (or a video game developer) will not lead to karmic ripening,[4] but killing an illusory being that has an illusory mind—that is, another sentient being—is a misdeed (verse 11). These two are different because the spells and the other tricks of an illusionist (or game developer) do not have the capacity to produce an illusory being that has subjective awareness (verse 12). All relative phenomena are products of many causes and conditions, but they do not arise when any one of the necessary causes is missing (verse 13ab). For consciousness, one of those necessary causes is a previous moment of consciousness. Matter and consciousness are fundamentally different in substance (one material, the other clear awareness), and matter cannot produce consciousness on its own.[5] Spells and technology are therefore not enough on their own to produce subjective awareness, so the illusions they produce are qualitatively different than sentient beings. In the case of actual sentient beings, the victim, the pain of being killed, the killer, and the malicious intent are ultimately all illusions, but neither the victim nor the killer realize that, and the act of killing thus continues the illusory cycle of karmic cause and effect in relative truth.

The last objection from the Foundation vehicle is that if the nature of sentient beings is emptiness—the ultimate truth, or nirvana—and yet they still wander in samsara, then buddhas would also transmigrate (cycle from one birth to the next), and trying to achieve buddhahood would be pointless (verses 13c–14b).

Shantideva responds that as long as the conditions that produce samsara—ignorance and craving—continue, beings experience the illusion of samsara without realizing that it is a fiction. But when those conditions have been severed and completely stop, the illusions of samsara will cease and those beings will achieve buddhahood, never to regress to samsara (verses 14c–15b).

Mind Only Objections to the Two Truths

Shantideva next addresses objections from the Mind Only school. As mentioned at the beginning of the chapter, the Mind Only school holds that all the appearances of relative phenomena are only mind but that mind itself must ultimately exist. Its proponents reason that when we perceive or think of an external object, such as a cup, we do not actually see the object but instead see a cognitive image of it—a picture in our mind—and no object can be proven to exist independent of that image.[6] Thus when the mind perceives an object, it is actually perceiving itself but mistaking it for an external object. Still, it cannot be denied that we have experience. The mind knows and is aware, but the cognitive image that it knows is nothing other than mind itself. The Mind Only school therefore says that the mind must exist in ultimate truth and that it is self-aware and self-illuminating, like a lamp flame.

The main difference between the Mind Only and the Middle Way positions is therefore whether the mind ultimately exists or not. Shantideva examines this in a dialogue in which the Mind Only proponent first objects that if mind did not exist, nothing could observe the illusions of relative truth. Therefore, the mind must exist, but everything it experiences is a cognitive image, which is nothing other than mind (verses 15cd–16).[7] Shantideva replies by explaining that when we analyze mind, we cannot actually prove its existence (verses 17–22), a position that he will lay out in greater detail later in the chapter. His principal objection to the Mind Only position is that if the mind were real, it could not be both the agent that performs an action and the object of that same action. Thus, as said in the *Sutra Requested by Ratnachuna*, mind cannot see itself—it cannot be both the seer and the seen. Shantideva also disposes with the analogies that the Mind Only school gives for a self-aware mind—a lamp that illuminates itself or the color blue whose blueness, they say, does not depend on other conditions. Whether described as luminous, self-aware, or otherwise, since the mind cannot be found when examined, there is no more point to discussing it than to speaking of the daughter of a childless woman, who of course cannot exist.

Another objection from the Mind Only school is that we can remember an experience only if our mind was aware of it at the moment we had it, and we can be aware of an experience only if the cognition of that experience is aware of itself. Otherwise, if another cognition were necessary to know that experience, then another would be necessary to know that second cognition, and yet another to know that one, ad infinitum, and we would never actually have any knowledge of the experience. Therefore, the fact that we remember experiences proves that mind is self-aware, they say (verse 23). Shantideva's response is that the memory of a prior experience arises from causes and conditions that are connected to that experience. He illustrates this by comparing it to the venom of a rat—which is perhaps a premodern way of conceptualizing the bacteria and other pathogens in a rat's saliva. As some Sanskrit commentators explain it, when a rat bites someone, its venom enters the body but the toxic effects do not become apparent until later, when it is activated by some condition, such as the sound of thunder. Similarly, even without self-awareness to plant an imprint of an experience, it is remembered later due to conditions. Self-awareness is thus unnecessary.

The Mind Only also says that the mind must exist because yogis who have the telepathic ability to perceive others' minds (called "other conditions" in verse 24) can see it. Shantideva replies that it is like people who put a magic eye salve on their eyes that lets them see treasure vases buried under ground. Even though they see the vases, they cannot see the salve on their eyes.

Likewise, although telepathic yogis perceive others' minds, they cannot perceive their own.

Although he refutes the view that mind or external objects exist ultimately, Shantideva is careful to point out that he is not denying that we see or know things—he is not denying experience. Instead, he is refuting our attachment to our experiences and the things we experience by refuting its basis, the attachment to them as real (verse 25). The Middle Way view is not a nihilistic view; emptiness does not mean an inert void. Instead, it means that what appears substantial, real, and enduring to us is in fact a constant flux of interdependent conditions. By realizing that there is nothing solid to grasp on to, we can overcome the attachments and cravings that cause our sufferings.

The next six lines (verses 26–27b) deal with a subschool of the Mind Only, the False Image school. This school posits that not only are external objects dreamlike and chimerical, cognitive images (called "illusions" in the verse) also do not truly exist, even though the mind itself does. Shantideva points out that it is logically inconsistent for the cognitive image (which the Mind Only holds to be mind) to be unreal while the mind itself is real. If the illusion or image seen is not real, then the mind that perceives it cannot be real either.

Though the Mind Only believes that a self-aware mind must exist to provide a real basis for experience (verse 27cd), there could be no relation between a real mind and unreal samsara (verse 28). When the mind no longer clings to any such focus or idea that it is apprehending anything, then the meditator sees that all phenomena are inseparable from the nature of the tathagatas, and there is no benefit to thinking everything is mind (verse 29).

The Fruition of Meditating on the Illusoriness of Appearances

When the Middle Way teaches that the path to liberation is to meditate on the illusoriness of all appearances, some opponents object that this is not an effective way to stop the afflictions, the main cause of suffering. They illustrate this with the analogy of an illusionist who creates the illusion of a lover and then feels lust for it, despite knowing that it is an illusion (verse 30).

Shantideva's response is that merely knowing that appearances are illusory is not enough. Every action we take, emotion we feel, and perception we have makes an imprint on our being. We have been habituated to the imprints of the afflictions since beginningless time, and the imprint of emptiness is weak in comparison (verse 31). By meditating on the idea that all phenomena are illusory, bodhisattvas will see that everything is emptiness; no true thing can be seen. As they integrate that realization more deeply into their being, the imprint of clinging to things as real will be diminished and eventually erased (verse 32ab). At first, this involves meditating that nothing exists, but that thought as well will be abandoned later (verse 32cd) because just as no thing can be seen, likewise no nothingness can be seen either. The idea of nothing depends upon the idea of a thing, so if there are no things at all, there cannot be any nothing either (verse 33). Seeing that there is neither thing nor nothing, bodhisattvas transcend all conceptual dualities of existent and nonexistent, permanent and impermanent, and so forth. Eventually, they see the true nature of all phenomena in its entirety and awaken to the utter peace of buddhahood, the nondual wisdom of a buddha (verse 34).

The life story of the Buddha relates how he passed away at the age of eighty-one and entered parinirvana, never to return to samsara. We might assume that this means that he entered the deep sleep of the grave and ceased to exist, but the Buddhist scriptures explain it otherwise. According to the teachings of the Foundation vehicle, at the moment of his death, the Buddha entered what is called the "absorption of cessation," a deep meditative state from which he need never arise. Suffering and its causes are extinguished, but wisdom is not. According to the Mahayana, however, buddhas in their great compassion would not remain in such a deep state of absorption, as they would be unable to help suffering beings. Instead, they transcend the extremes of both samsara and nirvana and perform activity to benefit sentient beings even as they dwell continually in meditation on nondual wisdom. They do this in different forms called *kayas* (the Sanskrit word for *body*), which arise due to the karma of their disciples and the aspirations that they themselves made before awakening (verse 35cd).

In this passage, Shantideva does not detail the nature of the kayas or explain buddha activity in detail. Instead, he briefly illustrates with analogies how the kayas and activity are thought-free and appear continuously. As in chapter 3, verse 20, Shantideva compares buddha activity to the wish-fulfilling jewel of a universal emperor and the heaven tree that gives the gods all that they wish for to illustrate how it is thought-free (verse 35ab). The long duration of buddha activity is shown through the analogy of a pillar with a capital in the shape of a garuda (a powerful bird that eats snakes and naga spirits). Its builder, the yogi Shanku, blessed the pillar through his meditation, giving it the ability to cure diseases caused by nagas for many years after he passed away. Similarly, once bodhisattvas have followed the path and awakened to buddhahood, they continue acting for the sake of all sentient beings effortlessly and spontaneously for a long time (verses 36–37).

One aspect of buddha activity is to serve as an object of veneration to which sentient beings can make offerings and thus gather merit (through positive habituation of their mind stream) by training in faith and generosity. The act of offering affects the worshipper's mind stream even though the buddhas have no mind (no dualistic thoughts or perceptions) of their own, and its results are experienced by both a Mahayana practitioner who sees the buddhas as illusory and a Foundation vehicle practitioner who considers the buddhas to truly exist (verses 38–39).

The Legitimacy of the Mahayana

Historically, the Mahayana only spread widely several centuries after Buddha passed into nirvana. By this time, the Foundation vehicle had codified its scriptures and considered them to be records of all the teachings the Buddha gave in his lifetime. Thus from its initial appearance, the Mahayana has been challenged by traditionalists, who attack it on two fronts. The first is to argue that the Foundation vehicle scriptures are sufficient on their own: they present a complete path to nirvana that many meditators have followed, eliminating all the afflictions and becoming arhats. The second is to deny that the Mahayana sutras were taught by the Buddha, and by extension, to deny that the Mahayana is Buddhism.

Shantideva weaves his responses to these two issues together. He first presents an objection from the Foundation vehicle: meditating on emptiness is unnecessary since one can achieve liberation by meditating on the four noble truths and seeing their nature. Shantideva responds that without an understanding of emptiness, it is impossible to achieve liberation. The Mahayana sutras teach that even realizing the four noble truths requires a degree of realization of emptiness (verse 40) and that the realization of the truths is in fact a partial realization of emptiness.

This argument leads into the issue of whether the Mahayana sutras are legitimate. Shantideva's position is that the Mahayana scriptures have authority for the same reasons that the Foundation vehicle scriptures have it: they are included in the sutras and vinayas (the two major categories of the Buddha's words) and do not contradict the nature of phenomena or the Buddha's teachings. Addressing the first, Shantideva points out the logical flaws in his opponent's argument. If the Foundation vehicle sutras are the words of the Buddha because followers of both the Foundation vehicle and Mahayana accept them, this would mean that when the followers of the Foundation vehicle were little children who had not yet been taught what the sutras are, neither the Foundation vehicle nor the Mahayana could be proven to be the words of the Buddha (verse 41). He also states that neither being accepted by two parties nor being under dispute can prove or disprove whether a scripture was taught by the Buddha (verses 42–43). Otherwise, non-Buddhist scriptures such as the Hindu Vedas would be Buddhist texts.

He next addresses the issue of whether the Mahayana teachings contradict the Buddha's teachings and the nature of phenomena. It is said in the scriptures that bhikshus—fully ordained monks and nuns—are the foundation of the teachings, but the scriptures teach that there are several types of bhikshus, including the true, or ultimate, bhikshu. Being such a bhikshu requires conquering the afflictions, which only a buddha has done completely, for that requires eliminating even the subtle fixation of the mind focusing on objects, and such fixation can be eliminated only by realizing emptiness (verse 44).

Shantideva also argues that if such liberation came solely from discarding the afflictions, then one would be fully liberated immediately upon discarding the afflictions. But there are stories of great arhats who, though they have achieved nirvana, are still subject to the ripening of karma, such as Maudgalyayana, the Buddha's great arhat disciple who was murdered by non-Buddhists (verse 45). The Foundation vehicle position is that arhats are subject to karma until their bodies pass away and their minds enter the absorption of cessation, but they are free of all craving and will therefore never take birth again. Shantideva responds that arhats may lack afflicted craving such as desire for gain and pleasure, but they still have unafflicted craving such as the wish to eat (verse 46). Craving arises out of feeling, which they still experience because they have the fixation of a mental focus of attention (verse 47). Though their mind might cease when they enter the absorption of cessation on achieving nirvana, it will rearise at some point, just as it does for non-Buddhists who practice the conception-free absorption, a state of dhyana meditation where there is no movement of mind at all. He therefore advises all who want to achieve liberation to meditate on emptiness (verse 48).

For Shantideva, the similarities between the Mahayana and Foundation vehicle teachings are so great that they outweigh any differences (verses 49–50). However, the teachings of the Mahayana are vast and profound, and even Mahakashyapa and Shariputra, who are recognized as some of the Buddha's greatest disciples, did not understand them (verse 51). That does not prove that the Mahayana sutras are not the Buddha's words, for not everyone who heard the Buddha teach understood everything that he said.[8]

Shantideva describes the Mahayana teachings on emptiness as the great medicine that cures the suffering of samsara (verses 52–55). It works by eliminating the causes of suffering, the two veils or obscurations mentioned in verse 54: the afflictive obscurations (the afflictions and the imprints they create in our mind stream) and the cognitive obscurations (the habits of dualistic conceptualization and their imprints). Far from being something to be afraid of, emptiness allows the bodhisattva to remain in samsara to work tirelessly for the sake of others.

METHODS FOR MEDITATING ON EMPTINESS

Having established the general outline of the two truths and the purpose for meditating on emptiness, Shantideva now presents the actual contemplations, the meditations on the lack of a self. In the Mahayana, these meditations are presented on two levels. The first is the selflessness of the individual, proving that there is no real self, or me, to be found in our body or mind. The second is the selflessness of phenomena, proving the emptiness of the phenomena that are the basis for thinking me or other. The selflessness of the individual is an idea common to all schools of Buddhism; the selflessness of phenomena is specific to the Mahayana.

Meditating on the Selflessness of the Individual

One of the basic teachings of Buddhism is that all our stresses and sorrows originate from clinging to a me, when in actuality, there is no me or self: we merely project the idea of an individual self onto our bodies and minds, leading to suffering and fear (verse 56). This is called "ego-clinging," and there are said to be two levels of it: the instinctive and the imaginary. Instinctive ego-clinging is the innate sense of a me that all sentient beings have, even babies or

244 — A CONTEMPORARY GUIDE

insects, who can be seen to act for their self-preservation. Imaginary ego-clinging refers to philosophical or religious ideas of a soul, or *atman*, that must be learned. These two are related, but they are often treated separately, as Shantideva does here.

Shantideva first examines instinctive ego-clinging (verses 57–59). Because our idea of me is based upon our body and mind, he examines their constituents to see if any me can be found. He first goes through his body parts, seeing that none of them can be identified as himself. He then examines his mind, which in Buddhism is considered to be an amalgam of six different consciousnesses—the five sensory consciousnesses and the sixth (mental) consciousness, or thinking mind. As all six are intermittent, none of them could be a true self, or the me would be constantly popping in and out of existence. If there were some other me to which the body parts and consciousnesses belonged, it would be logical for it to appear, for otherwise we would be entirely hidden to ourselves. But no such me can be found, no matter how hard we look for it. Our idea of me is a fiction that we project on our body and mind, sometimes seeing them as me and sometimes as mine. In reality, there is nothing there; it is an illusion.

Following this, Shantideva addresses imaginary ego-clinging, the ideas of a soul taught by non-Buddhist schools. He begins with the ideas of the Samkhya school. At the heart of the Samkhya system is the idea of a primal substance, a mixture of the three *gunas* (strands or qualities) called *rajas*, *tamas*, and *sattva*. When these are out of balance, they manifest through a three-step process as everything that is experienced.[9] What experiences them is the *purusha* (individual), a permanent, conscious self that always has the nature of awareness of sound and so forth. This is the point where Shantideva begins his argument, in verse 60, developing a line of reasoning that he briefly described in chapter 6, verses 27–28.

Shantideva argues that if the conscious self were permanent and perceived sound, then it must always hear sound, for otherwise it would not be conscious when it does not hear sound (verses 60–61). He also argues that a single, permanent cognition could not sometimes see form and sometimes hear sounds, for then it would change and necessarily be impermanent. The Samkhyas say that when the conscious self hears sound, it is cognition of sound, and when it sees form, it is cognition of form. They compare this to the way a person can be a parent in relation to one person and a child in relation to another or the way an actor can play one role in the matinee and another in the evening. Shantideva argues that in neither case could such a self be a singular, permanent consciousness because it changes dependent upon causes and conditions. Shantideva sarcastically remarks that if it were one, such oneness would have no precedent (verses 62–66). Moreover, it would follow that the sentient self and the nonsentient primal substance would be one and the same thing and all people would be one (verse 67).

Following the refutation of the Samkhya, Shantideva examines the Nyaya school's conception of an *atman*, or soul. The Nyaya posit that there is an unmoving and unchanging self that is not itself conscious. Instead, when consciousness arises, it is linked to this unchanging self in a temporary, accidental relation called a *conjunction* (hence the word *conjoined* in verse 68).[10] Shantideva has little patience for this idea. A self that is not sentient is little different from a jug or a blanket, and if it knows through a conjunction with sentience, it is difficult to say that it is still nonsentient (verse 68). Likewise, an unchanging self could never be affected by sentience; it would be little different from empty, inert space (verse 69).

One common objection to the Buddhist teachings on selflessness (here voiced from the perspective of the Vaisheshika school, which, like the Nyaya, posits that the soul is unchanging and unmoving) is that if there were no self, there could be no karmic cause and effect (verse 70). Shantideva replies that both Buddhists and the Vaisheshika accept that the body and mind (called the "bases" in verse 71) are different at the time of action and result, but if there were an unchanging self, it could not act upon either of them. Instead, when the Buddha taught that beings reap the results of acts they committed in the past, this was in terms of the moment-by-moment continuum of a mind stream (verse 72). The mind at the moment of the action acts as the cause of the immediately following moment, which then causes another and so on in a chain that continues through the time of the result. One might think that the continuum is a real self, but that cannot be because the past mind is gone and does not exist and the future mind has not yet come into existence. If the present mind were a me, that me would disappear when the present passes by in every instant (verse 73).

In verse 74, Shantideva addresses the Buddhist Vatsiputriya school, a Foundation vehicle school. The Vatsiputriya takes the view—unique among Buddhists—that there is an individual self but it is ineffable and cannot be described as either the same as, or different from, the body or mind. Shantideva likens this to the trunk of a banana tree, which looks as solid as any tree trunk from the outside. But as you peel back its layers, you see that it is actually the stalks of the leaves wrapped around each other, with no heartwood in the center. Similarly, you cannot find a me, ineffable or not, no matter how hard you scrutinize your continuum.

Another objection to selflessness is that without a self, meditating on compassion would be pointless because there would be no one to feel compassion for. But sentient beings have not realized selflessness and project the idea of a me out of delusion, causing themselves suffering. Thus bodhisattvas feel compassion for them, accepting their existence on the relative level in order to meditate on compassion and progress down the path to the result: buddhahood (verse 75). Although this thought is deluded, it is a useful fiction that motivates bodhisattvas to practice meditation on relative and ultimate bodhichitta and achieve the result (verse 76). It is different from ordinary ego-clinging in that it brings a positive result. Though stopping ego-clinging completely may seem difficult, meditating on or cultivating selflessness is the supreme meditation that uproots our grasping onto either an instinctive sense of me or a learned, imaginary idea of a soul (verse 77).

Meditating on the Selflessness of Phenomena

While the meditation on the lack of an individual self can eliminate ego-clinging and free us from our individual suffering, it does not remove all the cognitive obscurations of dualistic thought that prevent us from achieving our full potential for benefiting all sentient beings, buddhahood. For this reason, bodhisattvas also need to practice the meditation on emptiness, the selflessness of phenomena, which Shantideva presents as the four foundations of mindfulness: the mindfulness of body, feelings, mind, and phenomena. In these meditations, bodhisattvas use their strong mindfulness and awareness to allow their prajna to carefully examine the nature of phenomena without distraction.

The foundation of mindfulness of body begins in a similar fashion to the meditation on the selflessness of the individual, but instead of looking for an individual self, it involves looking for the body either in the individual body parts (verses 78–79) or as a whole that inhabits the various body parts, either externally in its physical form or internally in the consciousness (verses 80–82). Just as when he searched for a self, Shantideva cannot identify anything that can be called a body. Instead, he explains that we project the idea of a body onto its various parts from delusion, which is similar to mistaking a scarecrow for a human from afar (verse 83). For as long as the parts of the body are assembled, from the time they form a fetus in the womb until they disintegrate after death, they seem to be a body, but in reality, that is just a thought (verse 84).

Even when we realize that the whole body is a fiction, we might think that its parts exist, so Shantideva then dissects those into smaller and smaller parts until he sees that even atoms cannot truly exist as singular, indivisible, partless entities (verses 85–86).[11] This meditation is not merely an intellectual exercise: realizing that the body is merely an illusory conceptual projection negates our habit of feeling lust for attractive bodies and aversion toward ugly ones (verse 87), allowing us abandon the attachment and craving that cause our suffering.

The second of the four foundations is mindfulness of feelings—pleasant, unpleasant, and neutral sensations, either mental or physical. A feeling that truly exists would be enduring and not dependent upon conditions, but feelings are transient and dependent on other things—the body, mind, object, and so forth. Thus feelings cannot exist in suchness, even in a subtle form that is covered by a stronger opposite feeling (verses 88–90). Conceiving of pleasure and pain as real feelings is mere fixation that bodhisattvas should counter by meditating on its antidote (verses 91–92). These investigations become stronger with the powerful meditation of the first dhyana (which the verse calls "The dhyana that grows in the field of analysis"), a particular meditative state in which the mind is virtuous, clear, stable, and endowed with a capacity for incisive analysis.

After examining feelings themselves, Shantideva then examines their primary cause, the contact between the sensory faculty and object. He observes that contact is illogical when there is a gap between the faculty and the object, but he also argues that were there no gap, the partless, indivisible atoms would have to merge in order for there to be contact, as otherwise they would have parts—sides that touch and sides that do not (verses 93–95). Just as there can be no contact between atoms, there also can be no contact between an immaterial consciousness and a material object (verse 96). He thus determines that there is no actual contact between sensory faculties and objects. Since the contact that is its cause is illusory, feeling itself is also an illusion, and all our travails of seeking out pleasurable feelings and avoiding pain are pointless (verse 97). When the bodhisattva truly realizes and internalizes this, then the craving born from feelings will also cease, breaking the cycle of suffering (verse 98). Shantideva concludes this passage with three verses describing how feelings and the experience of them are illusory and thus incapable of causing any harm in actuality (verses 99–101).

When reading this passage from a modern perspective, we must remember that the ancients did not have the technical or mathematical apparatus of contemporary science. They did not conceive of light as photons or waves or of sounds as vibration in the air. Instead, they assumed that the eye actually saw the object, not light reflected from it, and they thought that sound was its own category of form. They had no concept of subatomic forces and assumed that if atoms did not touch, other atoms could pass between them and nothing would be solid. But the explanations given by physics do not necessarily contradict Shantideva's basic position that the contact of object and sensory faculty is illusory, and may in fact support it. Indeed, some contemporary thinkers make similar arguments.[12]

The third foundation of mindfulness is mindfulness of mind. Examining where and what the mind is, Shantideva observes that it cannot be found in the sensory faculties, their objects of form and so forth, or anywhere else (verse 102). If mind were real, then it would be either the same as the body or separate from it, but it cannot be established as either, so its nature is nirvana, beyond all conceptual elaboration (verse 103). The Buddhist scriptures teach that mind arises from a focus on its object, which acts as a condition, but both the objects and mind arise and perish in every single moment. If the object happens in one moment and the awareness of it in the next, then the object has perished and no longer exists when the awareness of it occurs, so the awareness cannot actually apprehend it. Similarly, if the mind precedes the object, the object has not yet come into being and cannot be known. If they occur at the same time, there can be no relation between the two (verses 104–5b), either causal or in terms of their identity. In this way, the mind and all phenomena are emptiness, naturally pure from the very beginning.

The fourth foundation of mindfulness is mindfulness of dharmas. The word *dharma* usually refers to the Buddha's teachings, but it can also mean "phenomena," which is the meaning intended here. In demonstrating that the body, feelings, and mind lack any nature, Shantideva has already established that all phenomena are emptiness—they cannot logically arise, and if they do not arise, they cannot truly exist (verse 105cd). Yet realists object that if there were no relative phenomena, there would be no relative truth, contradicting the teaching that there are two truths. Furthermore, if the relative is posited in relation to some other phenomenon, like a mirage mistaken for water, then there are no sentient beings and no one could reach nirvana (verse 106). Shantideva's response is that for the buddhas, there is neither ultimate nor relative truth; they have transcended all conceptions of true and false, being and not being, samsara and nirvana, and so forth. Saying that they are "buddhas" is a thought that other beings have about them, not their (the buddhas') own idea (verse 107). When yogis on the path arise from meditation and later recognize such a thought, the relative would exist from their perspective. After awakening to buddhahood, they dwell in thought-free wisdom beyond all extremes and have no conception of any relative phenomena existing. Still, they are able to realize nonconceptually how things appear interdependently to ordinary beings and thus they feel unbearable compassion for them.

Another objection is that if thoughts and the objects of thought are presented in relation to one another, then all logic and analysis would be impossible, for what would be examining what? Shantideva's response is that for the Middle Way, all reasoning is done according to the common consensus of how things appear to ordinary people (verse 108). It does not lead to an infinite regress because once a misconception has been dispelled by analysis, no further analysis is necessary. All projections and denials naturally cease, and the bodhisattva sees the luminous empty nature of all phenomena called the ultimate nirvana (verses 109–10).

ELIMINATING ATTACHMENT TO THINGS

Shantideva segues from the preceding discussion about the relation between analysis and the object of analysis into a broader examination of how entities cannot be proven to exist. He examines this first by investigating the relation between mind and what it knows. Generally, entities can be proven to exist only if they can be validly known, either by perception or reasoning. But the act of knowing depends upon there being something to know. Thus neither knowing nor the object of knowing can occur without one another—neither has independent existence, similar to how the labels of "parent" and "child" are given in relation to one another (verses 111–13). If being a child were an inherent part of someone's nature, they would be a child in relation to everyone. Instead they are called a "child" in relation to some people and "parents" in relation to others—"parent" and "child" are just projections we create depending upon conditions. An opponent might object that it is not like that: the cognition proves the existence of the known object, much as the presence of a shoot proves the prior existence of a seed. But Shantideva points out that this case is different because it is the knower itself that is in question. If there had to be another knower to know the first, then there would an infinite regress (verses 114–15). Thus there can be no valid proof that things exist independently.

Shantideva turns next to the vajra-splinter argument, a classic Middle Way form of reasoning. It takes its name from the god Indra's indestructible weapon, the vajra: just as a vajra is unstoppable, so too is this reasoning—one of the most powerful proofs of emptiness. This logic refutes that any thing can arise, on the grounds that it does not arise from itself, from something other than itself, from both itself and something other than itself, or without any cause at all. If something does not arise, it cannot truly exist and must therefore be emptiness.

Shantideva first observes that there is a common consensus that the sequence of cause and result is seen and known, so one cannot say things arise without any cause (verses 116–17). But then the question arises: is that cause other than what arises, or is it the same? Shantideva starts with the former—that things arise from something other than themselves. He has already refuted that things arise from other, ordinary things in the discussion of the four foundations of mindfulness above, so here he addresses the idea that the world and its inhabitants are created by an all-powerful god.

Specifically, he refutes the Vaisheshika view that there is a creator god who is an eternal, single, immaculate deity who is worthy of worship. Some Vaisheshikas identify that god with the elements of earth, water, fire, air, and space, but as Shantideva observes, that contradicts their description of God (verses 118–20). Moreover, Vaisheshikas hold that the atoms of the elements, and the self, like God, are permanent, so there is no way that they could be created. Cognition and sensations come from objects, not God, so it is unclear what their God could actually create (verses 121–22b).

Beginning with the second couplet of verse 122, Shantideva refutes the position that a creator god could be permanent and still produce results, an argument that would apply to any eternal supreme deity. If it is permanent, a producer such as God must always be producing all results at the same time or must never be producing any. If it produced some results at one time and other results at another, it would be changing from moment to moment and thus be impermanent. Such a God must depend either upon conditions or upon His own desires. In either case, He has no true autonomy and can hardly be almighty (verses 123–25).

The Hindu schools whose creator deity Shantideva refutes do not conceive of God as a judgmental deity like the Christian God. Instead, they largely accept that beings' rebirths are dictated by karma, though their conceptions of what that means diverge. This largely saves them from having to consider the problem of evil that has vexed Christian theologians—how a loving, omniscient, and omnipotent God could create a world in which there is evil, pain, and suffering—or the conundrum of why a loving God would create beings that He (being omniscient) knew would fall into hell. Though we can only speculate about what arguments Shantideva might have made, it seems likely that he would not have had much time for an appeal to free will as a defense of the existence and goodness of God, given his descriptions in the sixth chapter of sentient beings' lack of control over themselves.

In the first couplet of verse 126, Shantideva briefly dismisses the idea that permanent atoms could be the causes of things, a position of the Mimamsa and other schools, by noting that he has already refuted the true existence of atoms.[13] This completes his refutation of the position that things could arise from something other than themselves.

Shantideva next examines whether things arise from themselves, particularly in the manner described by the Samkhya school. As mentioned above in the discussion of the selflessness of the individual, the Samkhyas hold that things are the manifestation of a primal substance that consists of the three qualities sattva, rajas, and tamas (verses 126c–27). But if the primal substance is single, it is illogical for it to have three qualities (verse 128). Turning to the phenomena that the Samkhyas propose are manifestations of that primal substance, Shantideva refutes the views that sounds and so forth are produced by the elements and that pleasant or unpleasant feelings exist in external objects and are permanent (verses 129–34b). He then specifically refutes the Samkhya assertion that the result exists in its cause in an unmanifest form—for example, a clay jug exists in the lump of raw clay before the potter shapes it. The Samkhya posit this because they consider it impossible for the nonexistent to arise (verse 134). But Shantideva points out that when the potential jug is in the clay, no manifest instance of a jug exists, so for one to arise amounts to the same thing as the nonexistent arising (verse 135ab). He further dismisses the idea that the result is present in its cause by telling his opponents that they should wear cotton seeds instead of cotton cloth, remarking sarcastically that even Samkhya masters "who know reality" do not see cotton seeds as cloth (verses 135c–37).

The Samkhyas respond by saying that this criticism also applies to the Middle Way. If what is being evaluated is false, then the result of that analysis must also be false. Thus emptiness cannot be proven, and meditating on it is illogical, they say (verse 138). Shantideva replies that emptiness cannot be found anywhere else than in the imagined things of relative truth, the mere appearances that sentient beings cling to as true. Emptiness is merely their nature and cannot be found by any other method than examining them.

254 — A CONTEMPORARY GUIDE

Meditating on emptiness brings the realization that appearances are illusory and fictitious, counteracting clinging to reality. However, the idea that they are nonexistent is also fictitious, just as the death of a child in a dream is no more real than its birth, for the idea of nonexistence depends upon an idea of existence and the idea of unreality depends upon an idea of reality. Either extreme is a conceptual construct, not the true nature (verses 139–40). Shantideva closes this passage on the vajra-splinter argument by summarizing how it proves that when we examine their causes, we see that things are no different than illusions (verses 141–42).

Shantideva next turns to another classic Middle Way argument, the logic of analyzing the result to determine whether things exist at the time they arise or not. After teaching that what causes produce do not come from anywhere or go anywhere and are thus illusory (verses 143–44), he presents the crux of this logic: something that exists has no need of a cause, for it already exists, and something that does not exist can have no need of a cause because the nonexistent cannot need anything (verse 145). The existent cannot be transformed into the nonexistent and vice versa, and therefore there is no way that anything existent can arise or cease (verses 146–49). Thus all appearances are like illusions, empty of substance but arising as mere interdependent appearances; neither samsara nor nirvana can be observed to exist (verses 150–51).

The Results of Meditating on Emptiness

Shantideva closes the chapter with a lyrical description of the benefits of meditating on emptiness. He describes how once we realize emptiness, we cannot be carried away by afflictions because we are unmoved by worldly concerns and understand the nature of our likes and dislikes (verses 151–53). Yet at the same time, the realization of emptiness makes it clear how ordinary beings suffer pointlessly because of their delusion. Shantideva expresses this in a heartrending passage describing the pains sentient beings experience in samsara (repeatedly referred to as "existence" and "there") due their ignorance and misdeeds, unaware of how they are creating their own misery and unable to escape it (verses 154–65). The chapter concludes with a plaintive pair of stanzas in which Shantideva asks rhetorically when he will be able to bring comfort and happiness to beings and guide them to enlightenment (verses 166–67). The last stanza also implicitly teaches the path: bodhisattvas must gather the accumulations of merit and wisdom to free themselves of all dualistic focus (which entails fixation) and awaken to buddhahood. Only then will they gain the ability to help sentient beings overcome fixation and see the luminous, empty nature of suchness.

10. Dedication: Transcending Our Limited Vision

In Mahayana Buddhism, it is said that the ability of the buddhas and bodhisattvas to help sentient beings comes from the aspirations and dedications that they made in the past. Thus dedicating the virtue we do to the benefit of all sentient beings is considered an important conclusion to any meritorious activity. If we do so, in the future, when we become buddhas or high-level bodhisattvas ourselves, we will be able to benefit others in a vast and spontaneous way. If we do not, there is a danger that we might lose control of our mind and do something that cancels our meritorious act, such as act out of anger. As the Buddha said in the *Sutra Requested by Sagaramati*, dedicating merit to the enlightenment of all is like putting a drop of water into a great ocean. Just as that drop will not dry out until the entire ocean has dried up, the virtues we dedicate will not be exhausted until we reach buddhahood. For these reasons, Shantideva concludes the *Way of the Bodhisattva* with a long dedication of the merit of writing the work to the benefit of all sentient beings.

Beyond the scriptural reasoning, we can also see in our lives that when we pause after completing a good act, appreciate that it was good, and then dedicate it to bring even more good for all, that dedication reinforces the positive impact of the act. In particular, when the dedication is connected to our own experience, it can create more feeling and affect us more strongly. Yet our experience is limited, and left to our own devices, our dedications might be subconsciously limited by our own biases and preconceptions. Thus it is common practice among Buddhists to recite aspirations from the sutras or by great masters such as Shantideva, contemplating the words, joining them with their own experience, and making these masters' dedications their own.

This chapter opens with a general dedication for all sentient beings. Shantideva first plays on the words of the title to make the aspiration that all sentient beings enter the path to enlightenment (verse 1). He then makes the wish that all sentient beings may be happy and free of mental and physical suffering (verses 2–3). The first stanza is a wish for long-term benefit, and the next two a wish for happiness and relief from any suffering now.

DEDICATIONS FOR BEINGS IN THE LOWER REALMS

This general dedication is followed by a series of aspirations that the beings in the different realms of samsara be freed from the specific sufferings they experience. First among them are the dedications for the beings who suffer the tortures of the hells (verses 4–15). Buddhist scriptures describe numerous hell realms, each with their own agony, that are formed by the power of karma and experienced by their inhabitants as being as solid as the human world seems to us. There are hot hells where hell beings are burned by fire, cold hells where they freeze, and occasional hells with their own specific agony. In one, beings chased by savage dogs rush toward a forest seeking cool shade, only to be sliced by the sword-like leaves of the trees; in another, they see their lovers on the other side of a thick forest and struggle to join them only to be pierced by the long, iron thorns of the *shalmali* trees (verse 6). In the hell of the crushing mountains, beings are crushed repeatedly between large mountains that smash together (verse 8). The inhabitants of the hells experience the pain of dying, only to be revived and experience the same agony over and over again. When he contemplates their suffering, Shantideva feels such great compassion that he prays that all these tortures be transformed into delightful experiences, such as the Unfordable River of hell becoming the River Mandakini in heaven (verse 10).

Because the hells appear due to beings' karma, no one can directly rescue anyone else from them. But what perpetuates the suffering of the hells is the hatred in the hell beings' minds. When a bodhisattva such as Vajrapani, Padmapani (another name for Avalokiteshvara, the bodhisattva of compassion), Manjughosha, or Samantabhadra appears to the hell beings (verses 11–15), a positive feeling of faith may arise within the hell beings, interrupting the hatred and allowing them the relief of dying and being reborn in a higher realm. Those beings may think it is the blessing of the bodhisattvas that frees them; in actuality, it is the pure sincerity of a feeling of faith.

For Shantideva, the sufferings of hell are as real as the suffering in any realm. Though they are illusory in nature, the beings caught in them do not realize that and experience the torments as if they were real, much as we experience the human realm. As taught in chapter 5, in Buddhism, these tortures are not considered punishment by a wrathful god; they are products of karma that "arise from wicked thoughts" (chap. 5, verse 8). Acting on a hateful intention plants a seed of hatred that quietly festers in the mind stream until the conditions are ready for it to ripen as a horrifying, painful experience of hell. When it does, the being who performed the act that caused it has long since perished, and the being who now experiences the result deserves compassion as much as anyone else who experiences suffering. There is no judgment, only the wish to free them of their agonies.

Shantideva next makes an aspiration on behalf of the animals (verse 16ab). His specific aspiration is for animals to be free of the fear of being eaten, but this is representative of the wish that they be free of any type of suffering, including that of being enslaved, confined in crowded cages or pens, and butchered. Shantideva also prays that the hungry ghosts, who are tormented by never-ending hunger and thirst, may experience pleasures equal to that of the humans on the northern continent of Unpleasant Sound, where, according to traditional Buddhist cosmology, humans lead delightful thousand-year lives with little suffering (verse 16). He also wishes that they be able to receive the compassion of great bodhisattvas such as Avalokiteshvara, called by the name Lokeshvara in the verse (verse 17).

DEDICATIONS FOR HUMANS

Just as he dedicates his merit to benefit beings in the lower realms, Shantideva also dedicates it to the benefit of humans. This begins with aspirations that those who experience suffering be freed of their sorrows (verses 18–26). This includes the sufferings of physical difficulties, poverty, despondency and mental illness (verse 20cd), and so forth. He prays that women may be freed of the types of suffering that primarily affect them, such as the pain of childbirth. He illustrates this by referring to the Buddha's mother Queen Maya-devi, who gave birth completely painlessly in the grove of Lumbini (verse 18cd). All of these prayers are about broad categories of suffering that would have been evident to all at Shantideva's time; we can use these as examples of sufferings that we see humans experience, either with our own eyes or through what we learn in the media.

Merely being free of suffering now is not enough; beings also need to be prosperous and have the resources they need for practicing dharma (verses 27–41). This includes the ability to remember past lives (verse 27), which can be developed from meditation, so that humans will understand cause and effect and refrain from misdeeds. Spiritual practice requires leisure time and resources, so Shantideva prays that all may be as wealthy as if they had mastered the samadhi called the "treasury of the sky" (verse 28), through which whatever the meditator wishes for appears from the sky. Shantideva also prays that women may be reborn in favorable positions where they can practice dharma, as women of his day were considered the property of their fathers or husbands and had little self-determination and fewer opportunities to practice dharma.[1] Likewise those with low status have difficulty finding time to practice; he prays that they achieve good social standing and yet be free of any pride that would cause them to abuse their new status. He prays that the world may be like a pure realm where the ground is as smooth as *vaidurya*, a translucent volcanic glass or beryl (verse 35), and that all beings live in an environment so conducive to dharma practice that even flesh-eating demons such as dakinis and raksha-sas are filled with compassion (verse 40).

DEDICATIONS FOR DHARMA PRACTITIONERS

Shantideva next dedicates the virtue so that dharma practitioners of all levels may have all they need to progress in their practice. In particular, he prays that the members of the sangha, the bhikshus and bhikshunis (fully ordained monks and nuns), be well supported, have good conditions, and keep their vows (verses 42–45). He prays that all sentient beings achieve a precious human body, which is superior to a god's body because it is conducive to dharma practice (verse 47), and subsequently gather merit and come to the state of buddhahood (verse 48). He then aspires that all the types of noble individuals fulfill their aspirations, including buddhas, bodhisattvas, pratyeka-buddhas (beings who because of the strength of their merit and practice in previous lifetimes, achieve enlightenment without serving a teacher in their last lifetime), and shravakas (disciples of the Buddha who follow the teachings of the Foundation vehicle).

Shantideva then dedicates the virtue so that he may progress along the path and achieve the first bodhisattva level, called Joyous (verse 51), which is the stage when a bodhisattva first directly sees the empty nature of all phenomena. He prays that he may always be able to follow Manjushri, the bodhisattva who was his special deity, and also emulate him in deeds and aspirations (verses 52–56). Lastly, he dedicates the merit so that the teachings of Buddhism may long remain (verse 57) and concludes the chapter and his work by recalling the kindness of Manjushri and his spiritual teachers and bowing to them in homage (verse 58).

In Tibet, this chapter is considered one of the great aspiration prayers collectively known as "The Five Aspirations." It is often recited on its own, either as a dedication prayer to close a group puja or service, or in an individual's own practice. Many people, both monastic and lay, recite it on a regular basis (often from memory) to dedicate the merit of whatever virtuous action they have done. Shantideva's vast, expansive aspirations have provided both an inspiration and a model for generations of Buddhist practitioners, helping them go beyond the limitations of their ordinary ways of thinking and make genuine dedications to become able to relieve all sentient beings of the myriad sufferings they experience. As Shantideva says in a verse frequently cited by the Dalai Lama and other masters:

> For as long as space endures,
> As long as there are beings,
> I will remain to eliminate
> The sufferings of beings. (chap. 10, verse 55)

Like any great work, the *Way of the Bodhisattva* has many layers of meaning—more than can be explained in a short guide such as this. Its most important lessons become clear only with reflection, meditation, and experience over time. Above all, it is a text whose teachings are meant to be put into practice. Doing so will, at the very least—and this is by no means a small thing—help us become better people, which is the basis for any spiritual practice. Finding yourself becoming more generous, more compassionate, less easily angered, and more peaceful are signs that Shantideva's words have begun to wend their way from your head to your heart. It is my hope that my translation of the *Way of the Bodhisattva* and this contemporary guide will help make it possible for Shantideva's words to find their way into the thoughts and hearts of all who read them, benefiting them in some way, no matter how it may manifest. To paraphrase Shantideva,

> By the merit of my translating
> The *Way of the Bodhisattva*,
> May every wandering being enter
> The bodhisattvas' ways.
> *And so on ...*

Resources for Further Study

AS INTEREST IN the *Way of the Bodhisattva* has grown in the English-speaking world, many Buddhist teachers, notably His Holiness the Dalai Lama, have taught the text regularly, and many books about it have been published. Though it is not possible to give an exhaustive list, a few representative choices are listed here.

Several of His Holiness the Dalai Lama's teachings on the *Way of the Bodhisattva* have been published in English. His recent title *The Bodhisattva Guide: A Commentary on "The Way of the Bodhisattva"* (translated by the Padmakara Translation Group and published by Shambhala Publications in 2018) stands out as an excellent introduction to Shantideva's work and demonstrates why this work is so revered in the Tibetan tradition. For many readers, Pema Chödrön's *Becoming Bodhisattvas: A Guidebook for Compassionate Action* (published by Shambhala Publications in 2018) will give the most practical guide to incorporating Shantideva's teachings into their lives. One of the most well-regarded Tibetan commentaries is Khenpo Kunzang Pelden's *Nectar of Manjushri's Speech* (translated by the Padmakara Translation Group and published by Shambhala Publications in 2011). This commentary gives a word-by-word explanation of the text and is recommended for people who want to study the text in more depth. An alternate translation of the first five chapters of this commentary is available online at www.kunpal.com.

The ninth chapter has traditionally received the greatest attention from commentators, and there are several books specifically on this chapter in English. As one would expect, the Dalai Lama's

Practicing Wisdom: The Perfection of Shantideva's Bodhisattva Way (translated and edited by Geshe Thupten Jinpa and published by Wisdom Publications in 2005) is a clear and accessible teaching connecting the understanding of emptiness to the larger issue of how to be a good human being. The commentary by Mipham Rinpoche, published in English as *The Wisdom Chapter: Jamgön Mipham's Commentary on the Ninth Chapter of "The Way of the Bodhisattva"* (translated by the Padmakara Translation Group and published by Shambhala Publications in 2017) is a renowned presentation of Nyingma interpretation of Middle Way thought and also includes a lengthy discussion of the differences between the Nyingma and Geluk presentations of the Middle Way. Finally, Karl Brunnhölzl's *The Center of the Sunlit Sky: Madhyamaka in the Kagyü Tradition* (published by Snow Lion Publications in 2004) contains a translation of Pawo Rinpoche's commentary on this chapter, which served as the basis for my own presentation here.

ABBREVIATIONS

DK   Derge Kangyur, electronic version found at
        Adarsha, https://adarsha.dharma-treasure.org
        /home/kangyur.

Pañjikā Prajñākaramati. *Bodhicāryāvatāra pañjikā* (*Byang
        chub kyi spyod pa la 'jug pa'i dka' 'grel*). Translated
        by Sumatikīrti, Mar pa chos kyi dbang phyug, and
        Gnyan dar ma grags. Derge Tengyur, dBu ma la,
        folios 41b–288a.

Pawo   Pawo Tsuglak Trengwa (dPa' bo gtsug lag phreng
        ba). *Byang chub sems dpa'i spyod pa la 'jug pa'i
        rnam par bshad pa theg chen chos kyi rgya mtsho zab
        rgyas mtha' yas pa'i snying po zhes bya ba bzhugs so.*
        Varanasi: Vajra Vidya Library, 2003.

GLOSSARY

abbot. The senior monastic who presides over ordination ceremonies and then instructs new monks and nuns in learning how to live the monastic life.

afflictions (Skt. *kleshas*). The mental events of desire, aversion, ignorance, pride, stinginess, envy, and so forth that motivate actions that perpetuate samsaric suffering.

arhat. An individual who has eliminated all the afflictions and thus liberated themselves from samsara, achieving nirvana. This result is the ideal of the Foundation vehicle schools.

awareness. 1. The quality of knowing what is happening in your body, speech, or mind at any given moment. 2. A synonym for cognition or mind.

bhikshu. A fully ordained Buddhist monk.

bhikshuni. A fully ordained Buddhist nun.

bodhisattva. A being who has taken the vow to achieve buddhahood for the sake of all beings.

carefulness. The quality of valuing karmic cause and effect so greatly that one is careful to avoid misdeeds and practice virtue to the greatest extent possible.

chakravarti. In Indian lore, an emperor who peacefully rules over one or more continents, overcoming enemies by the mere display of strength.

demigods. A class of beings who live on the slopes of Mount Meru and are consumed with envy for the gods who live on the peak.

dharma. A buddha's or other noble being's realization of the nature of the truth, the expression of that in words, and by extension, the teachings of Buddhism.

dhyana. A particular technique of mental absorption that leads to withdrawal from the sensory world and entry into subtle states of consciousness.

Foundation vehicle. The initial teachings given by the Buddha to his disciples, which emphasize discipline and the lack of an individual self.

four foundations of mindfulness. Meditations on the nature of the body, feelings, mind, and dharmas, or phenomena. They are called "foundations of mindfulness" because they are based on strong mindfulness.

garuda. A mythical bird that eats naga spirits and poisonous snakes.

going forth. The traditional term for going forth from home to homelessness and becoming ordained as a monastic.

higher realms. The realms of humans, demigods, and gods, where beings enjoy the temporary pleasures of samsara.

hungry ghost. A being who, due to the power of karma, lives for thousands of years suffering from terrible hunger and thirst, unable to find anything to eat or drink.

insight meditation. Meditation whose primary aim is to see the nature of reality, realizing the right view.

Jambudvipa. The continent that, according to traditional Buddhist cosmology, lies to the south of Mount Meru. It corresponds to present-day South Asia, the land where the Buddha appeared and taught the dharma, and is sometimes used as a synonym for the world.

Jataka tales. The stories of the previous lives of Buddha Shakyamuni.

levels. Also called the "bodhisattva levels." The ten stages of realization that bodhisattvas progress through from the time they first realize the nature of phenomena until they reach buddhahood.

lower realms. The realms of hells, animals, and hungry ghosts, where sufferings predominate and pleasures are rare.

Mahayana. The Buddhist school that emphasizes the motivation of bodhichitta and the practices of a bodhisattva.

maras. Malevolent spirits personifying our attachments and preventing us from attaining the results of Buddhist practice.

Middle Way. A Mahayana school that refutes any idea of existence or nonexistence, since any idea of a thing existing or not is merely a conceptual fabrication that prevents us from seeing the actual nature of phenomena.

Mimamsa. A non-Buddhist school that emphasizes the proper practice of Brahmanic ritual.

Mind Only. A Mahayana school that asserts that external phenomena are projections of the mind, but that mind itself truly exists.

mindfulness. The ability to recall what one should do or not do, or alternatively, the ability to remember the instructions of the teacher.

Mount Meru. The great mountain at the center of the world, according to traditional Buddhist cosmology.

nirvana. The state of liberation from samsara, where all suffering and afflictions are extinguished.

Nyaya. An Indian non-Buddhist school that shares many positions with the Vaisheshika. It is known for its system of logic and epistemology.

obscurations, two. Afflictive obscurations (the afflictions and the imprints they create in our mind stream) and the cognitive obscurations (the habits of dualistic conceptualization and their imprints).

prajna. The ability to distinguish what is dharma and should be done from what is not dharma and should be given up.

pratyekabuddhas. Beings who achieve enlightenment without following a teacher in their final lifetime. Their realization is said to be higher than that of a listener arhat but still incomplete.

primal substance. According to the Samkhya school, the source out of which all phenomena arise and appear to the self.

sage (Skt. *muni*). An epithet for the buddhas, so called as they have stilled all the obscurations of body, speech, and mind.

Samkhya. One of the oldest and most influential Indian non-Buddhist philosophical traditions.

sangha. The monastic order of Buddhist monks and nuns, or those bodhisattvas who have directly seen the empty nature of phenomena and achieved the bodhisattva levels.

shamatha. A type of meditation that trains the mind in resting without being distracted by thoughts or the appearances of external things.

shravakas. The Buddha's early disciples who practice the teachings of the Foundation vehicle, and their followers.

sugata. An epithet for the buddhas, literally meaning "gone excellently," as the buddhas' realization surpasses that of other beings and is irreversible.

tathagata. An epithet for the buddhas, literally meaning that they have gone to or realized suchness, the nature of all things.

transcendences, six (Skt. *paramita*). Transcendent generosity, discipline, patience, diligence, meditation, and prajna. The Sanskrit *paramita* means "gone beyond"; these qualities are so called because they transcend ordinary, worldly generosity and so forth.

Vaisheshika. An Indian non-Buddhist tradition that has a strong realist tendency and classifies all phenomena into six categories.

Vatsiputriya school. A Foundation vehicle Buddhist school that, uniquely among Buddhist schools, posits that the self of an individual exists as an ineffable entity.

veils. See **obscurations, two**.

victor. An epithet for the buddhas, who are victorious in the struggle over the four maras.

Notes

Translator's Preface

1. These evaluations of the literary qualities of Shantideva's verse are based mostly upon the Tibetan translation, as my reading knowledge of Sanskrit is not sufficient to judge the literary merits of the extant Sanskrit on its own.

2. I also consulted the article by Luis Gómez, "The Way of the Translators: Three Recent Translations of Śāntideva's *Bodhicaryāvatāra*," *Buddhist Literature* 1 (1999): 262–354.

3. A comparative study of the meters of the Sanskrit and the Tibetan translations might be an interesting topic for research, but it is beyond the scope of this project and the skills of this translator, who has no formal training in Sanskrit meters.

4. Recordings of the Sanskrit are available at Bodhisvara: Melodies of Awakening, www.bodhisvara.com.

5. The majority of the translation is set in loose iambic tetrameter or common meter for Shantideva's *anushtubh* or the Tibetan seven-syllable lines. Longer lines are set in pentameter, alexandrines, or even longer meters, corresponding to the line length in the Sanskrit and Tibetan. Most of the irregularities are extra unstressed syllables in some feet, such as are found in the work of poets such as Blake or Yeats, though with more frequency. There are also two passages in the ninth chapter where the meter was changed to a longer line even though there was no meter change in either the Sanskrit or the Tibetan.

6. As in chap. 9, v. 79, for example.

Introduction

1. For those who are interested in more in-depth explanations, a short list of recommended works for further study is also included at the end of this book.

2. Much of the ninth chapter of Pawo's commentary has been translated by Karl Brunnhölzl in *The Center of the Sunlit Sky: Madhyamaka in the Kagyü Tradition* (Ithaca, NY: Snow Lion Publications, 2004), but the entire commentary has not yet been translated into English.

3. Skt. *hinayana.*

4. This number seems to have been rounded up; the canonical text actually has 915 stanzas.

5. Giving up the kingdom and teaching the *Way of the Bodhisattva* are the first two of the seven wondrous tales. The remaining tales relate how Shantideva resolved a conflict in the east; fed five hundred people with wrong views in a famine, thus converting them all to Buddhism; fed one thousand beggars in a famine; served as a bodyguard for a king with a wooden sword that shone bright light; and engaged in a contest with a non-Buddhist teacher who had drawn a mandala in the sky, destroying the mandala and converting all present to Buddhism.

6. Atisha Dipamkara was said to have studied this work with Dharmakirti Suvarnadvipa in Sumatra. Pawo, p. 1:20.

7. Pawo, 1:31. The figure 108 may not be literal and could mean a large number in general.

8. Several contemporary scholars have questioned the authenticity of the canonical version of the text, primarily because of the differences between the received text and the manuscript found in Dunhuang as well as a stylistic analysis of the extant Sanskrit. There is much discussion about whether some stanzas and passages in the received text might have been added later and are not Shantideva's own words. (Several of the suspect stanzas have been subjected to similar scrutiny in both the Tibetan and Sanskrit commentaries.)

9. Pawo Tsuglak Trengwa, for example, lists in his commentary several different lineages from which he received the transmission of the text, first among them the tradition that passed from Shantideva through several Indian masters to Dharmakirti Suvarnadvipa (known in Tibetan as Serlingpa) and Atisha Dipamkara, who brought this lineage to Tibet.

CHAPTER 1: BENEFITS

1. The extant Sanskrit text gives the title as *Bodhicaryāvatāra*, and many Western scholars frequently refer to the text by this shorter Sanskrit title. Though the word *bodhisattva* ordinarily has two *t*'s, the title in the canonical Tibetan gives it with an alternate spelling with only one *t*.

2. The homage is only two lines in Sanskrit and Tibetan but is translated into three lines in English.
3. Traditionally, it is taught that there are eight leisures and ten resources. They are described in many different texts, including Gampopa, *Ornament of Precious Liberation*, trans. Ken Holmes, ed. Thupten Jinpa (Somerville, MA: Wisdom Publications, 2017), 25–34; Jamgön Kongtrul Lodrö Thaye, *The Torch of True Meaning*, trans. David Karma Choephel (Woodstock, NY: KTD Publications, 2014), 5–10; and Patrul Rinpoche, *Words of My Perfect Teacher*, trans. Padmakara Translation Group, rev. ed. (Boston: Shambhala Publications, 1978), 19–37, among others.
4. According to Buddhist cosmology, there are an infinite number of universes. Each of them is formed due to the collective karma of sentient beings, endures for billions of years, and then is destroyed by fire, water, and wind. After a period of time, a new universe will again form, and the cycle will repeat.
5. The story is recounted in full in Padma Choe-phel, *Leaves of the Heaven Tree: The Great Compassion of the Buddha*, trans. Deborah Black (Berkeley: Dharma Publishing, 1997), 407–11.

CHAPTER 2: CONFESSION

1. This division into seven is according to Pawo Tsuglak Trengwa. Some commentaries say that there are eight branches, counting prostration (which Pawo considers an aspect of offering) as a separate practice.
2. Though one would normally say "take refuge" in English, the traditional formulation of "going for refuge" stresses that finding refuge is an active process. One must actually put the teachings of Buddhism into practice in order to receive any protection from them.

CHAPTER 3: EMBRACING BODHICHITTA

1. In the early nine-chapter translation into Tibetan found in Dunhuang, these two chapters are combined into a single chapter. See Kate Crosby and Andrew Skilton, trans., *The Bodhicaryāvatāra: A Guide to the Buddhist Path to Awakening* (Birmingham: Windhorse Publications, 2004), xl–xlii.
2. Vasubandhu, *The Treasury of Abhidharma*, chap. 8, v. 41.
3. To rouse bodhichitta on their own, practitioners recite first the stanza of going for refuge "Until enlightenment, I go for refuge" (chap. 2, v. 26) and then these two verses, repeating the three stanzas three times.

CHAPTER 4: CAREFULNESS

1. DK, mdo sde pha, folios 94b–95a.
2. *Ārya-kusumasañcayā-nāma-mahāyāna-sūtra*, DK, mdo sde 'a, folio 302ab.

CHAPTER 5: AWARENESS

1. Though generosity is not given its own chapter, it is described in several passages throughout the text, including in the offerings at the beginning of the second chapter; the dedications in the third chapter, where Shantideva gives his body, belongings, and virtues to all sentient beings; and later on in this chapter, where he discusses the discipline of benefiting sentient beings.
2. DK, 'bum ga pa, folio 179a.
3. In tantric Buddhism, the flesh-eating dakinis mentioned here would be considered worldly dakinis. There are also wisdom dakinis, enlightened beings appearing in a semiwrathful female form.
4. As cited in *Pañjikā*, folio 95b.
5. This idea will be explained in depth in chapter 9.
6. The Buddha made a rule that monks and nuns should not give away the three dharma robes—the external signs of a monastic—because people would not recognize a monk or nun who was not wearing them as being a monastic.
7. *Buddhāvataṃsakasūtra*, sangs rgyas phal po che'i mdo, phal chen a, folios 281ff.
8. The *Compendium of the Sutras* may have been translated into Tibetan, but it is not included in the standard canon, the Tengyur, and may well have been lost.

CHAPTER 6: PATIENCE

1. DK, 'dul ba nga, folio 20a.
2. As cited in Pawo, 1:589–90.

CHAPTER 7: DILIGENCE

1. As cited in Pawo, 2:38.

CHAPTER 8: MEDITATION

1. DK, 'dul ba ca, folio 20.

2. Peter Alan Roberts, trans., *King of Samādhis Sūtra*, chap. 36. 84000: Translating the Words of the Buddha, http://read.84000.co/translation/UT22084-055-001.html.

3. Supushpachandra is traditionally said to have been reborn as the bodhisattva Chandraprabha at the time of the Buddha and later as the twelfth-century Tibetan master Gampopa.

4. Dharmakirti (tenth century CE) was the teacher of Atisha and a principal figure in the Indian transmission of the *Way of the Bodhisattva* into Tibet. In Tibetan, he is usually called Serlingpa ("the one from Suvarnadvipa"). He is not to be confused with the Dharmakirti, the fourth-century master famed for his teachings on logic and epistemology.

5. Cited in Pawo, 2:161.

CHAPTER 9: PRAJNA

1. "The impulse of the Vaiśeṣika system is derived from its hostility to Buddhistic phenomenalism." S. Radhakrishnan, *Indian Philosophy*, Vol. 2., 2nd ed. (Delhi: Oxford University Press, 2008), 157.

2. Radhakrishnan, 347.

3. In this verse, some read the Tibetan word for mind, *blo*, as referring to intellect or conceptual mind. But if that were so, then nonconceptual perceptions (such as when the eye sees a cup) would perceive the ultimate truth, which verse 6 clearly refutes. Further, the Sanskrit uses the word *buddhi*, which frequently is used for sensory perception in other treatises, including the works of Dharmakirti. Thus, it is clear that Shantideva here intends all dualistic cognition, not merely thought or intellect.

4. Though it may habituate the mind to killing.

5. According to Buddhist theories of causation, results arise from a substantial cause and cooperating conditions. The substantial cause must be a preceding instance of the same substance as the result, though the cooperating causes may be of any type. Since consciousness is clear awareness in substance, its substantial cause must also be clear awareness—a preceding instant of consciousness. Therefore, there is no way that matter alone can produce consciousness without a preceding moment of consciousness to act as the substantial cause.

6. We cannot prove that any object exists independently of our mind because proving existence requires that we validly apprehend the object, whether perceptually or inferentially, and we cannot apprehend an object without using our mind. Thus any time we prove a thing's existence, there is necessarily a cognitive image of it. Objects can therefore never be observed separately from the cognitive images of them and cannot be proven to exist separately from them. Therefore, external objects must be the same in substance as the cognitive images. Since cognitive images are clearly mental, external objects are therefore mind.

7. To be more precise, the Mind Only school asserts that there are actually two cognitive images: an apprehended image (the image of the object that is seen) and an apprehending image (the feeling of being aware of perceiving the apprehended image). The latter is what the phrase "there is something else" in verse 16 refers to, according to the *Pañjikā*.

8. Several commentators dispute the authenticity of verses 49–51, explaining that they must not be Shantideva's own words because their tone is demeaning to the opponents and they occur out of order. Pawo Rinpoche insists that they are indeed Shantideva's words, but he orders the verses differently, placing these three stanzas after verse 43b.

9. The three steps are called *buddhi* (intellect), *ahamkara* (egoity), and *manas* (mind).

10. The Sanskrit word for conjunction is *samyoga*, though in the verse it is shortened to simply *yoga*. This contraction of the word is also seen in other philosophical works, such as Dharmakirti's *Commentary on Validity* 3.173.

11. Even in contemporary physics, it is difficult to establish that fundamental particles are enduring things. The quantum theorist Carlos Rovelli writes that on the subatomic level "there is only the frenzied swarming of quanta that appear and vanish," a description that accords with Buddhist presentations of emptiness and subtle impermanence. *The Order of Time* (New York: Riverhead Books, 2018), 126.

12. As Robert Wright states, "We don't have much direct contact with the world; the things we see and smell are some distance from our bodies, so all the brain can do is make inferences about them based on indirect evidence." *Why Buddhism Is True: The Science and Philosophy of Meditation and Enlightenment* (New York: Simon and Schuster, 2017), 144.

13. Atoms are refuted in chap. 9, v. 86.

CHAPTER 10: DEDICATION

1. The original text reads as a prayer that women be reborn as men. In ancient Buddhist literature, there is little or no discussion of the idea that the society could be changed so that women could enjoy equality and the leisure to practice that would bring. In that context, a prayer to be reborn as a man would have been seen as a prayer to be reborn in a position where one would have more freedom to practice the dharma. Hence it is rendered in this translation as a rebirth in a favorable position rather than in a male body.

BIBLIOGRAPHY

VERSIONS OF SHANTIDEVA'S TEXT

This translation was prepared by comparing several different editions of the canonical Tibetan: a traditional pecha format published by the Sherig Parkhang in Dharamsala; electronic versions by Asian Classics Input Project, Adarsha, and the Vajra Vidya Library; the versions of the root text found in the commentaries listed below; and the critical edition found in volume 61 of the dPe bsdur ma edition of the Tengyur. I also consulted an electronic edition of the Sanskrit found at the Digital Sanskrit Buddhist Canon, http://www.dsbcproject.org/canon-text/book/258.

COMMENTARIES CONSULTED

Darma Rinchen (Dar ma rin chen). *Spyod 'jug rtsa 'grel bzhugs so.* Xining: mTsho sngon mi rigs due skrun khang, 1994.

Ju Mipham ('Ju mi pham). *Shes rab le'u'i tshig don go sla bar rnam par bshad pa nor bu ke ta ka zhes bya ba bzhugs so.* Sichuan: Si khron mi rigs due skrun khang, 1993.

Kunzang Pelden (Kun bzang dpal ldan). *Byang chub sems dpa'i spyod pa la 'jug pa'i tsig 'grel 'jam dbyang bla ma'i zhal lung bdud rtsi'i thig pa.* Varanasi: Nyingmapa Student Welfare Committee, 1999.

Pawo Tsuglak Trengwa (dPa' bo gtsug lag phreng ba). *Byang chub sems dpa'i spyod pa la 'jug pa'i rnam par bshad pa theg chen chos kyi rgya mtsho zab rgyas mtha' yas pa'i snying po zhes bya ba bzhugs so.* Varanasi: Vajra Vidya Library, 2003.

Pema Karpo (Kun mkhyen pad ma dkar po). *sPyod 'jug rtsa ba dang 'brel pa dbu ma'i lam gyi sgron me zhes bya ba bzhugs so.* Varanasi: Kargyud Relief and Protection Committee, 2002.

Prajñākaramati. *Bodhicāryāvatāra pañjikā.* Digital Sanskrit Buddhist Canon, http://www.dsbcproject.org/canon-text/book/553.

_____. *Byang chub kyi spyod pa la 'jug pa'i dka' 'grel.* Translated by Suma-
tikīrti, Mar pa chos kyi dbang phyug, and gNyan dar ma grags. Derge
Tengyur, dBu ma la, folios 41b–288a.

Vibhutichandra. *Byang chub kyi spyod pa la 'jug pa'i dgongs pa'i 'grel pa
khyad par gsal byed ces bya ba.* Derge Tengyur, dBu ma sha, folios
192b–285a.

OTHER TRANSLATIONS CONSULTED

Batchelor, Stephen, trans. *A Guide to the Bodhisattva's Way of Life.* Dharamsala: Library of Tibetan Works and Archives, 1979.

Crosby, Kate, and Andrew Skilton, trans. *The Bodhicaryāvatāra: A Guide
to the Buddhist Path to Awakening.* Birmingham: Windhorse Publications, 2004.

Gómez, Luis O., trans. *Introduction to the Practice of the Bodhisattva Path
(The Bodhicharyavatara).* In *The Norton Anthology of World Religions:
Buddhism,* edited by Donald S. Lopez Jr. New York: W. W. Norton,
2015, pp. 395–441.

Padmakara Translation Group, trans. *The Way of the Bodhisattva: A
Translation of the "Bodhicharyāvatāra."* Rev. ed. Boston: Shambhala
Publications, 2006.

Wallace, Vesna A., and B. Allan Wallace, trans. *A Guide to the Bodhisattva
Way of Life.* Ithaca, NY: Snow Lion Publications, 1997.

OTHER SOURCES CITED

Brunnhölzl, Karl. *The Center of the Sunlit Sky: Madhyamaka in the Kagyü
Tradition.* Ithaca, NY: Snow Lion Publications, 2004.

Gampopa. *Ornament of Precious Liberation.* Translated by Ken Holmes.
Edited by Thupten Jinpa. Somerville, MA: Wisdom Publications, 2017.

Gómez, Luis O. "The Way of the Translators: Three Recent Translations of
Śāntideva's *Bodhicaryāvatāra.*" *Buddhist Literature* 1 (1999): 262–354.

Jamgön Kongtrul Lodrö Thaye. *The Torch of True Meaning.* Translated by
David Karma Choephel. Woodstock, NY: KTD Publications, 2014.

Padma Choe-phel. *Leaves of the Heaven Tree: The Great Compassion of
the Buddha.* Translated by Deborah Black. Berkeley: Dharma Publishing, 1997.

Patrul Rinpoche. *Words of My Perfect Teacher.* Translated by the Padmakara Translation Group. Rev. ed. Boston: Shambhala Publications, 1978.

Radhakrishnan, S. *Indian Philosophy*. Vol. 2. 2nd ed. Delhi: Oxford University Press, 2008.

Roberts, Peter Alan, trans. *King of Samādhis Sūtra*. 84000: Translating the Words of the Buddha. https://read.84000.co/translation /UT22084-055-001.html.

Rovelli, Carlos. *The Order of Time*. New York: Riverhead Books, 2018.

Vasubandhu. *Verses on the Treasury of Abhidharma*. Translated by David Karma Choephel. In *Jewels from the Treasury: Vasubandhu's "Verses on the Treasury of Abhidharma" and Its Commentary "Youthful Play" by the Ninth Karmapa Wangchuk Dorje*. Woodstock, NY: KTD Publications, 2012.

Wright, Robert. *Why Buddhism Is True: The Science and Philosophy of Meditation and Enlightenment*. New York: Simon and Schuster, 2017.

INDEX

bodhichitta and, 159
bodhisattva vow and, 163
two truths and, 235
meritorious actions. *See* virtuous
actions
Middle Way school, 147, 149, 229, 233,
236, 238, 250, 251, 254
Milarepa, 168
Mimamsa school, 229, 230, 253
mind
as constantly changing continuum,
220–21
defined, 231
examining constituents of, 244, 249
foundation of mindfulness of, 249
gaining control over, 186–87,
190–91
self-awareness of, 237
solitude of, 218–19
Mind Only school, 229
two truths and, 236–38
mindfulness
developing, 187–89
diligence and, 212–13
five causes of, 188
importance of, 185–87
refraining from harmful actions and,
189–90
See also four foundations of
mindfulness
misdeeds
carefulness in resisting, 181
discipline of refraining from, 189–91
overcoming past, 159
ripening of karma and, 156, 166–67
motivation
bodhisattva vow and, 180
Mahayana and, 149

Nagarjuna, 229
Nalanda, university of, 147, 150
Nectar of Manjushri's Speech (Khenpo
Kunzang Pelden), 263
negative emotions, 181. *See also*
afflictions
Ngok Lotsawa Loden Sherap, 144, 151
nihilistic view, 233, 238

nirvana, requesting buddhas not to
pass into, 172–73
nonawareness, near affliction of, 190
Nyaya school, 200, 229, 230, 245

obscurations
cognitive, 247
elimination of, 159, 182, 188,
243, 247
to meditation, 224–25
offerings, making, 163–65, 240
to all sentient beings, 173
unexcelled offerings, 164
Ornaments of the Buddhas Sutra,
194, 210

Padmapani, 259
pain, patience and, 198–201
Patanjali, 229
patience, 177, 186–87, 197–205
of contemplating dharma, 199–200
offensive people and, 203–4
for overcoming anger, 197–98
with pain and harm, 198–201
of rejoicing in enemies' good
fortune, 202–3
results of practicing, 204–5
for those who harm loved ones,
201–2
when desires are frustrated, 203–4
Pawo Tsuglak Trengwa, 148,
272n9
perseverance, diligence and, 212–13
phenomena, emptiness of, 247–50
pleasure seeking, obscuration of, 224
*Practicing Wisdom: The Perfection
of Shantideva's Bodhisattva Way*
(Dalai Lama), 264
prajna (wisdom), 177, 186–87, 227–55
defined, 227–28
different schools of, 228–30
Foundation vehicle and, 233–36
illusoriness of appearances and,
238–40
meditating on emptiness and,
254–55
Mind Only school and, 236–38